THE MINISTRY OF HEALING FOR BLACK AMERICA

E. G. WHITE

FOY INSTITUTE PRESS

THE MINISTRY OF HEALING FOR BLACK AMERICA

ISBN 1-886002-15-0

CREDITS:
Cover Design by Square 1 Studio
Interior designed by Lee Cherry
Cover Photography by Marcus J.Wilson and Ronald Lytle

PUBLISHED BY
FOY INSTITUTE PRESS
P.O. Box 25
Hagerstown, Maryland 21741-0025
http://www.FOYPRESS.COM

Printed in U.S.A.

FOREWORD

NONE OF THESE DISEASES

"What mean ye, that ye use this proverb concerning [Black America] saying, The fathers have eaten sour grapes, and the children's teeth are set on edge?" *Ezekiel 18:12*

"And the Lord God planted a garden eastward in [Africa]... and commanded the man, saying, Of every tree of the garden thou mayest freely eat: But of the tree of the knowledge of good and evil, thou shalt not eat of it: for in the day that thou eatest thereof thou shalt surely die." *Genesis 2:8, 16-17*

"Grains, fruits, nuts, and vegetables constitute the diet chosen for us by our Creator. These foods, prepared in as simply and natural manner as possible, are the most healthful and nourishing. They impart a strength, a power of endurance, and a vigor of intellect that are not afforded by a more complex and stimulating diet."

The Ministry of Healing, p.90

For centuries, Satan has ingeniously sown the seeds of death in America. Blacks, dependent, fearful, and uninformed, have blindly cultivated a vineyard of "sour grapes" that has predisposed them to poor health. The complex and unresolved issues of Black health have produced a baleful harvest of physical disease and needless suffering, psychological pain and maladaptive behavior, religious deception and spiritual darkness; "And the children's teeth are set on edge."

Today, Blacks continue partaking of America's forbidden fruit by imitating the decadent values and lifestyles in White culture. These are the sour grapes that bring all manner of disease and moral decay. With limited health care coverage, declining resources and spiritual power, Blacks are forced to struggle, unaided, with chronic disease, psychological shame and spiritual apathy, "And the children's teeth are set on edge."

If Blacks learn no other lesson from history, let them understand that they must take responsibility for themselves. Too many Blacks, like Whites, take better care of their clothes and their cars, their houses and their pets, than the health of their own bodies. Many Black Christians take great pride in the beautiful churches they build for the praise and worship of God, yet the body-temple that God built and gave them for the indwelling of His Spirit is polluted with dead foods, toxic drinks, chemical additives, and all manner of unclean things. "What, know ye not that your body is the temple of the Holy Ghost which is in you, and ye are not your own?" *1Corinthians 6:19*

Black thought leaders (ie: parents, pastors and physicians; actors, activists, and administrators; editors, educators and entrepreneurs; citizens, commissioners and counselors) all must be enlisted to resolve the Black health crisis. Black leaders who adopt a healthy lifestyle, and utilize the resources at their command, can mobilize the moral and economic capital of Black institutions and the religious community for an effective collective response.

THE MINISTRY OF HEALING creates affordable HMOs (health ministry opportunity) for everyone, and can restore Black America's total health and true identity. Its message provides in simple language a comprehensive coverage of the practical instruction necessary for promoting health and preventing disease. It also reveals the moral incentive and spiritual power so essential for true and lasting change.

"In [these] days they shall say no more, The fathers have eaten a sour grape, and the children's teeth are set on edge. But every one shall die for his own inquitiy: every man that eateth the sour grape, his teeth shall be set on edge." *Jeremiah 31:29-30*

"If thou wilt diligently hearken to the voice of the Lord thy God, and wilt do that which is right in his sight and wilt give ear to his commandments, and keep all his statutes, I will put none of these diseases upon thee, which I have brought upon the [oppressors]: for I am the Lord that healeth thee." *Exodus 15:26*

The Publishers

TABLE of CONTENTS

OUR EXAMPLE

Our Lord Jesus Christ came to this world as the unwearied servant of man's necessity. He "took our infirmities, and bare our sicknesses," that He might minister to every need of humanity. Matthew 8:17. The burden of disease and wretchedness and sin He came to remove. It was His mission to bring to men complete restoration; He came to give them health and peace and perfection of character. Varied were the circumstances and needs of those who besought His aid, and none who came to Him went away unhelped. From Him flowed a stream of healing power, and in body and mind and soul men were made whole.

The Saviour's work was not restricted to any time or place. His compassion knew no limit. On so large a scale did He conduct His work of healing and teaching that there was no building in Palestine large enough to receive the multitudes that thronged to Him. On the green hill slopes of Galilee, in the thoroughfares of travel, by the seashore, in the synagogues, and in every other place where the sick could be brought to Him, was to be found His hospital. In every city, every town, every village, through which He passed, He laid His hands upon the afflicted ones and healed them. Wherever there were hearts ready to receive His message, He comforted them with the assurance of their heavenly Father's love. All day He ministered to those who came to Him; in the evening He gave attention to such as through the day must toil to earn a pittance for the support of their families.

Jesus carried the awful weight of responsibility for the salvation of men. He knew that unless there was a decided change in the principles and purposes of the human race, all would be lost. This was the burden of His soul, and none could appreciate the weight that rested upon Him. Through childhood, youth, and manhood He walked alone. Yet it was heaven to be in His presence. Day by day He met trials and temptations; day by day He was brought into contact with evil and witnessed its power upon those whom He was seeking to bless and to save. Yet He did not fail or become discouraged.

In all things He brought His wishes into strict abeyance to His mission. He glorified His life by making everything in it subordinate to the will of His Father. When in His youth His mother, finding Him in the school of the rabbis, said, "Son, why hast Thou thus dealt with us?" He answered,–and His answer is the keynote of His lifework,– "How is it that ye sought Me? wist ye not that I must be about My Father's business?" Luke 2:48, 49.

His life was one of constant self-sacrifice. He had no home in this world except as the kindness of friends provided for Him as a wayfarer. He came to live in our behalf the life of the poorest and to walk and work among the needy and the suffering. Unrecognized and unhonored, He walked in and out among the people for whom He had done so much.

He was always patient and cheerful, and the afflicted hailed Him as a messenger of life and peace. He saw the needs of men and women, children and youth, and to all He gave the invitation, "Come unto Me."

During His ministry, Jesus devoted more time to healing the sick than to preaching. His miracles testified to the truth of His words, that He came not to destroy, but to save. Wherever He went, the tidings of His mercy preceded Him. Where He had passed, the objects of His compassion were rejoicing in health and making trial of their new-found powers. Crowds were collecting around them to hear from their lips the works that the Lord had wrought. His voice was the first sound that many had ever heard, His name the first word they had ever spoken, His face the first they had ever looked upon. Why should they not love Jesus and sound His praise? As He passed through the towns and cities He was like a vital current, diffusing life and joy." See Matthew 4:15, 16, A.R.V., margin.

The Saviour made each work of healing an occasion for implanting divine principles in the mind and soul. This was the purpose of His work. He imparted earthly blessings, that He might incline the hearts of men to receive the gospel of His grace.

Christ might have occupied the highest place among the teachers of the Jewish nation, but He preferred rather to take the gospel to the poor. He went from place to place, that those in the highways and byways might hear the words of truth. By the sea, on the mountainside, in the streets of the city, in the synagogue, His voice was heard explaining the Scriptures. Often He taught in the outer court of the temple, that the Gentiles might hear His words.

So unlike the explanations of Scripture given by the scribes and Pharisees was Christ's teaching, that the attention of the people was arrested. The rabbis dwelt upon tradition, upon human theory and speculation. Often that which men had taught and written about the Scripture was put in place of the Scripture itself. The subject of Christ's teaching was the word of God. He met questioners with a plain, "It is written," "What saith the Scripture?" "How readest thou?" At every opportunity when an interest was awakened by either friend or foe He presented the word. With clearness and power He proclaimed the gospel message. His words shed a flood of light on the teachings of patriarchs and prophets, and the Scriptures came to men as a new revelation. Never before had His hearers perceived in the word of God such depth of meaning.

Never was there such an evangelist as Christ. He was the Majesty of heaven, but He humbled Himself to take our nature, that He might meet men where they were. To all people, rich and poor, free and bond, Christ, the Messenger of the covenant, brought the tidings of salvation. His fame as the Great Healer spread throughout Palestine. The sick came to the places through which He would pass, that they might call on Him for help. Hither, too, came many anxious to hear His words and to receive a touch of His hand. Thus He went from city to city, from town to town, preaching the gospel and healing the sick–the King of glory in the lowly garb of humanity.

He attended the great yearly festivals of the nation, and to the multitude absorbed in outward ceremony He spoke of heavenly things, bringing eternity within their view. To all He brought treasures from the storehouse of wisdom. He spoke to them in language so simple that they could not fail of understanding. By methods peculiarly His own, He helped all who were in sorrow and affliction. With tender, courteous grace He ministered to the sin-sick soul, bringing healing and strength.

The prince of teachers, He sought access to the people by the pathway of their most familiar associations. He presented the truth in such a way that ever after it was to His hearers intertwined with their most hallowed recollections and sympathies. He taught in a way that made them feel the completeness of His identification with their interests and happiness. His instruction was so direct, His illustrations were so appropriate, His words so sympathetic and cheerful, that His hearers were charmed. The simplicity and earnestness with which He addressed the needy, hallowed every word.

What a busy life He led! Day by day He might have been seen entering the humble abodes of want and sorrow, speaking hope to the downcast and peace to the distressed. Gracious, tenderhearted, pitiful, He went about lifting up the bowed-down and comforting the sorrowful. Wherever He went, He carried blessing.

While He ministered to the poor, Jesus studied also to find ways of reaching the rich. He sought the acquaintance of the wealthy and cultured Pharisee, the Jewish nobleman, and the Roman ruler. He accepted their invitations, attended their feasts, made Himself familiar with their interests and occupations, that He might gain access to their hearts, and reveal to them the imperishable riches.

Christ came to this world to show that by receiving power from on high, man can live an unsullied life. With unwearying patience and sympathetic helpfulness He met men in their necessities. By the gentle touch of grace He banished from the soul unrest and doubt, changing enmity to love, and unbelief to confidence.

He could say to whom He pleased, "Follow Me," and the one addressed arose and followed Him. The spell of the world's enchantment was broken. At the sound of His voice the spirit of greed and ambition fled from the heart, and men arose, emancipated, to follow the Saviour.

BROTHERLY LOVE

Christ recognized no distinction of nationality or rank or creed. The scribes and Pharisees desired to make a local and a national benefit of the gifts of heaven and to exclude the rest of God's family in the world. But Christ came to break down every wall of partition. He came to show that His gift of mercy and love is as unconfined as the air, the light, or the showers of rain that refresh the earth.

The life of Christ established a religion in which there is no caste, a religion by which Jew and Gentile, free and bond, are linked in a common brotherhood, equal before God. No question of policy influenced His movements. He made no difference between neighbors and strangers, friends and enemies. That which appealed to His heart was a soul thirsting for the waters of life.

He passed by no human being as worthless, but sought to apply the healing remedy to every soul. In whatever company He found Himself He presented a lesson appropriate to the time and the circumstances. Every neglect or insult shown by men to their fellow men only made Him more conscious of their need of His divine-human sympathy. He sought to inspire with hope the roughest and most unpromising, setting before them the assurance that they might become blameless and harmless, attaining such a character as would make them manifest as the children of God.

Often He met those who had drifted under Satan's control, and who had no power to break from his snare. To such a one, discouraged, sick, tempted, fallen, Jesus would speak words of tenderest pity, words that were needed and could be understood. Others He met who were fighting a hand-to-hand battle with the adversary of souls. These He encouraged to persevere, assuring them that they would win; for angels of God were on their side and would give them the victory.

At the table of the publicans He sat as an honored guest, by His sympathy and social kindliness showing that He recognized the dignity of humanity; and men longed to become worthy of His confidence. Upon their thirsty hearts His words fell with blessed, life-giving power. New impulses were awakened, and to these outcasts of society there opened the possibility of a new life.

Though He was a Jew, Jesus mingled freely with the Samaritans, setting at nought the Pharisaic customs of His nation. In face of their prejudices He accepted the hospitality of this despised people. He slept with them under their roofs, ate with them at their tables,–partaking of the food prepared and served by their hands,–taught in their streets, and treated them with the utmost kindness and courtesy. And while He drew their hearts to Him by the tie of human sympathy, His divine grace brought to them the salvation which the Jews rejected.

PERSONAL MINISTRY

Christ neglected no opportunity of proclaiming the gospel of salvation. Listen to His wonderful words to that one woman of Samaria. He was sitting by Jacob's well, as the woman came to draw water. To her surprise He asked a favor of her. "Give Me to drink," He said. He wanted a cool draft, and He wished also to open the way whereby He might give to her the water of life. "How is it," said the woman, "that Thou, being a Jew, askest drink of me, which am a woman of Samaria? for the Jews have no dealings with the Samaritans." Jesus answered, "If thou knewest the gift of God, and who it is that saith to thee, Give Me to drink; thou wouldest have asked of Him, and He would have given thee living water.... Whosoever drinketh of this water shall thirst again: but whosoever drinketh of the water that I shall give him shall never thirst; but the water that I shall give him shall be in him a well of water springing up into everlasting life." John 4:7-14.

How much interest Christ manifested in this one woman! How earnest and eloquent were His words! When the woman heard them, she left her waterpot, and went into the city, saying to her friends, "Come, see a man, which told me all things that ever I did: is not this the Christ?" We read that "many of the Samaritans of that city believed on Him." Verses 29, 39. And who can estimate the influence which these words have exerted for the saving of souls in the years that have passed since then?

Wherever hearts are open to receive the truth, Christ is ready to instruct them. He reveals to them the Father, and the service acceptable to Him who reads the heart. For such He uses no parables. To them, as to the woman at the well, He says, "I that speak unto thee am He."

CHRIST'S DAYS OF MINISTRY

In the fisherman's home at Capernaum the mother of Peter's wife is lying sick of "a great fever,"and "they tell Him of her." Jesus "touched her hand, and the fever left her," and she arose and ministered to the Saviour and His disciples. Luke 4:38; Mark 1:30; Matthew 8:15.

Rapidly the tidings spread. The miracle had been wrought upon the Sabbath, and for fear of the rabbis the people dared not come for healing until the sun was set. Then from the homes, the shops, the market places, the inhabitants of the city pressed toward the humble dwelling that sheltered Jesus. The sick were brought upon litters, they came leaning upon staffs, or, supported by friends, they tottered feebly into the Saviour's presence.

Hour after hour they came and went; for none could know whether tomorrow would find the Healer still among them. Never before had Capernaum witnessed a day like this. The air was filled with the voice of triumph and shouts of deliverance.

Not until the last sufferer had been relieved did Jesus cease His work. It was far into the night when the multitude departed and silence settled down upon the home of Simon. The long, exciting day was past, and Jesus sought rest. But while the city was wrapped in slumber, the Saviour, "rising up a great while before day," "went out, and departed into a solitary place, and there prayed." Mark 1:35.

Early in the morning Peter and his companions came to Jesus, saying that already the people of Capernaum were seeking Him. With surprise they heard Christ's words, "I must preach the kingdom of God to other cities also: for therefore am I sent." Luke 4:43.

In the excitement which then pervaded Capernaum there was danger that the object of His mission would be lost sight of. Jesus was not satisfied to attract attention to Himself merely as a wonder-worker or as a healer of physical disease. He was seeking to draw men to Him as their Saviour. While the people were eager to believe that He had come as a king to establish an earthly reign, He desired to turn their minds from the earthly to the spiritual. Mere worldly success would interfere with His work.

And the wonder of the careless crowd jarred upon His spirits. No self-assertion mingled with His life. The homage which the world gives to position, wealth, or talent was foreign to the Son of man. None of the means that men employ to win allegiance or command homage did Jesus use. Centuries before His birth it had been prophesied of Him, "He shall not cry, nor lift up, nor cause His voice to be heard in the street. A bruised reed shall He not break, and the dimly burning flax shall He not quench: He shall bring forth judgment unto truth." Isaiah 42:2, 3, margin.

The Pharisees sought distinction by their scrupulous ceremonialism and the ostentation of their worship and their charities. They proved their zeal for religion by making it the theme of discussion. Disputes between opposing sects were loud and long, and it was not unusual to hear on the streets the voice of angry controversy from learned doctors of the law.

In marked contrast to all this was the life of Jesus. In that life no noisy disputation, no ostentatious worship, no act to gain applause, was ever witnessed. Christ was hid in God, and God was revealed in the character of His Son. To this revelation Jesus desired the minds of the people to be directed.

The Sun of Righteousness did not burst upon the world in splendor, to dazzle the senses with His glory. It is written of Christ, "His going forth is prepared as the morning." Hosea 6:3. Quietly and gently the daylight breaks upon the earth, dispelling the darkness and waking the world to life. So did the Sun of Righteousness arise, "with healing in His wings." Malachi 4:2.

From Herod's dungeon, where in disappointment and perplexity concerning the Saviour's work, John the Baptist watched and waited, he sent two of his disciples to Jesus with the message:

"Art Thou He that should come, or do we look for another?" Matthew 11:3.

The Saviour did not at once answer the disciples' question. As they stood wondering at His silence, the afflicted were coming to Him. The voice of the Mighty Healer penetrated the deaf ear. A word, a touch of His hand, opened the blind eyes to behold the light of day, the scenes of nature, the faces of friends, and the face of the Deliverer. His voice reached the ears of the dying, and they arose in health and vigor. Paralyzed demoniacs obeyed His word, their madness left them, and they worshiped Him. The poor peasants and laborers, who were shunned by the rabbis as unclean, gathered about Him, and He spoke to them the words of eternal life.

Thus the day wore away, the disciples of John seeing and hearing all. At last Jesus called them to Him, and bade them go and tell John what they had seen and heard, adding, "Blessed is he, whosoever shall not be offended in Me." Verse 6. The disciples bore the message, and it was enough.

John recalled the prophecy concerning the Messiah, "Jehovah hath anointed Me to preach good tidings unto the meek; He hath sent Me to bind up the brokenhearted, to proclaim liberty to the captives, and the opening of the prison to them that are bound; to proclaim the year of Jehovah's favor, and ... to comfort all that mourn." Isaiah 61:1, 2, A.R.V. Jesus of Nazareth was the Promised One. The evidence of His divinity was seen in His ministry to the needs of suffering humanity. His glory was shown in His condescension to our low estate.

The works of Christ not only declared Him to be the Messiah, but showed in what manner His kingdom was to be established. To John was opened the same truth that had come to Elijah in the desert, when "a great and strong wind rent the mountains, and brake in pieces the rocks before the Lord; but the Lord was not in the wind: and after the wind an earthquake; but the Lord was not in the earthquake: and after the earthquake a fire; but the Lord was not in the fire:" and after the fire, God spoke to the prophet by a still, small voice. 1 Kings 19:11 12. So Jesus was to do His work, not by the overturning of thrones and kingdoms, not with pomp and outward display, but through speaking to the hearts of men by a life of mercy and self-sacrifice.

The kingdom of God comes not with outward show. It comes through the gentleness of the inspiration of His word, through the inward working of His Spirit, the fellowship of the soul with Him who is its life. The greatest manifestation of its power is seen in human nature brought to the perfection of the character of Christ.

The followers of Christ are to be the light of the world; but God does not bid them make an effort to shine. He does not approve of any self-satisfied endeavor to display superior goodness. He desires that their souls shall be imbued with the principles of heaven; then, as they come in contact with the world, they will reveal the light that is in them. Their steadfast fidelity in every act of life will be a means of illumination.

Wealth or high position, costly equipment, architecture or furnishings, are not essential to the advancement of the work of God; neither are achievements that win applause from men and administer to vanity. Worldly display, however imposing, is of no value in God's sight. Above the seen and temporal, He values the unseen and eternal. The former is of worth only as it expresses the latter. The choicest productions of art possess no beauty that can compare with the beauty of character, which is the fruit of the Holy Spirit's working in the soul.

When God gave His Son to our world, He endowed human beings with imperishable riches–riches compared with which the treasured wealth of men since the world began is nothingness. Christ came to the earth and stood before the children of men with the hoarded love of eternity, and this is the treasure that, through our connection with Him, we are to receive, to reveal, and to impart.

Human effort will be efficient in the work of God just according to the consecrated devotion of the worker–by revealing the power of the grace of Christ to transform the life. We are to be distinguished from the world because God has placed His seal upon us, because He manifests in us His own character of love. Our Redeemer covers us with His righteousness.

In choosing men and women for His service, God does not ask whether they possess worldly wealth, learning, or eloquence. He asks, "Do they walk in such humility that I can teach them My way? Can I put My words into their lips? Will they represent Me?"

God can use every person just in proportion as He can put His Spirit into the soul temple. The work that He will accept is the work that reflects His image. His followers are to bear, as their credentials to the world, the ineffaceable characteristics of His immortal principles.

"HE SHALL GATHER THE LAMBS WITH HIS ARM."

As Jesus ministers in the streets of the cities, mothers with their sick and dying little ones in their arms press through the throng, seeking to come within reach of His notice.

Behold these mothers, pale, weary, almost despairing, yet determined and persevering. Bearing their burden of suffering, they seek the Saviour. As they are crowded back by the surging throng, Christ makes His way to them step by step, until He is close by their side. Hope springs up in their hearts. Their tears of gladness fall as they catch His attention, and look into the eyes expressing such pity and love.

Singling out one of the group, the Saviour invites her confidence, saying, "What shall I do for thee?" She sobs out her great want, "Master, that Thou wouldest heal my child." Christ takes the little one from her arms, and disease flees at His touch. The pallor of death is gone; the life-giving current flows through the veins; the muscles receive strength. Words of comfort and peace are spoken to the mother; and then another case, just as urgent, is presented. Again Christ exercises His life-giving power, and all give praise and honor to Him who doeth wonderful things.

We dwell much on the greatness of Christ's life. We speak of the wonderful things that He accomplished, of the miracles that He wrought. But His attention to things accounted small is even higher proof of His greatness.

Among the Jews it was customary for children to be brought to some rabbi, that he might lay his hands upon them in blessing; but the disciples thought the Saviour's work too important to be interrupted in this way. When the mothers came desiring Him to bless their little ones, the disciples looked on them with disfavor. They thought these children too young to be benefited by a visit to Jesus, and concluded that He would be displeased at their presence. But the Saviour understood the care and burden of the mothers who were seeking to train their children according to the word of God. He had heard their prayers. He Himself had drawn them into His presence.

One mother with her child had left her home to find Jesus. On the way she told a neighbor her errand, and the neighbor wished to have Jesus bless her children. Thus several mothers came here together, with their little ones. Some of the children had passed beyond the years of infancy to childhood and youth. When the mothers made known their desire, Jesus heard with sympathy the timid, tearful request. But He waited to see how the disciples would treat them. When

He saw the disciples reproving the mothers and sending them away, thinking to do Him a favor, He showed them their error, saying, "Suffer the little children to come unto Me, and forbid them not: for of such is the kingdom of God." Mark 10:14. He took the children in His arms, He laid His hands upon them, and gave them the blessings for which they came.

The mothers were comforted. They returned to their homes strengthened and blessed by the words of Christ. They were encouraged to take up their burden with new cheerfulness and to work hopefully for their children.

Could the afterlife of that little group be opened before us, we should see the mothers recalling to the minds of their children the scene of that day, and repeating to them the loving words of the Saviour. We should see, too, how often, in after years, the memory of these words kept the children from straying from the path cast up for the ransomed of the Lord.

Christ is today the same compassionate Saviour as when He walked among men. He is as verily the helper of mothers now as when He gathered the little ones to His arms in Judea. The children of our hearths are as much the purchase of His blood as were the children of long ago.

Jesus knows the burden of every mother's heart. He who had a mother that struggled with poverty and privation, sympathizes with every mother in her labors. He who made a long journey in order to relieve the anxious heart of a Canaanite woman will do as much for the mothers of today. He who gave back to the widow of Nain her only son, and in His agony upon the cross remembered His own mother, is touched today by the mother's sorrow. In every grief and every need, He will comfort and help.

Let mothers come to Jesus with their perplexities. They will find grace sufficient to aid them in the care of their children. The gates are open for every mother who would lay her burdens at the Saviour's feet. He who said, "Suffer the little children to come unto Me, and forbid them not" (Mark 10:14), still invites mothers to bring their little ones to be blessed by Him.

In the children who were brought in contact with Him, Jesus saw the men and women who should be heirs of His grace and subjects of

His kingdom, and some of whom would become martyrs for His sake. He knew that these children would listen to Him and accept Him as their Redeemer far more readily than would grown-up people, many of whom were the worldly-wise and hardhearted. In teaching, He came down to their level. He, the Majesty of heaven, answered their questions and simplified His important lessons to meet their childish understanding. He planted in their minds the seeds of truth, which in after years would spring up and bear fruit unto eternal life.

When Jesus told the disciples not to forbid the children to come to Him, He was speaking to His followers in all ages –to officers of the church, ministers, helpers, and all Christians. Jesus is drawing the children, and He bids us, "Suffer them to come;" as if He would say, They will come, if you do not hinder them.

Let not your un-Christlike character misrepresent Jesus. Do not keep the little ones away from Him by your coldness and harshness. Never give them cause to feel that heaven would not be a pleasant place to them if you were there. Do not speak of religion as something that children cannot understand, or act as if they were not expected to accept Christ in their childhood. Do not give them the false impression that the religion of Christ is a religion of gloom, and that in coming to the Saviour they must give up all that makes life joyful.

As the Holy Spirit moves upon the hearts of the children, co-operate with His work. Teach them that the Saviour is calling them, that nothing can afford Him greater joy than for them to give themselves to Him in the bloom and freshness of their years.

PARENTAL RESPONSIBILITY

The Saviour regards with infinite tenderness the souls whom He has purchased with His blood. They are the claim of His love. He looks upon them with unutterable longing. His heart is drawn out, not only to the best-trained and most attractive children, but to those who by inheritance and through neglect have objectionable traits of character. Many parents do not understand how much they are responsible for these traits in their children. They have not the tenderness and wisdom to deal with the erring ones whom they have made what they are. But Jesus looks upon these children with pity. He traces from cause to effect.

The Christian worker may be Christ's agent in drawing these faulty and erring ones to the Saviour. By wisdom and tact he may bind them to his heart, he may give courage and hope, and through the grace of Christ may see them transformed in character, so that of them it may be said, "Of such is the kingdom of God."

FIVE SMALL BARLEY LOAVES FEED THE MULTITUDE

All day the people had thronged the steps of Christ and His disciples as He taught beside the sea. They had listened to His gracious words, so simple and so plain that they were as the balm of Gilead to their souls. The healing of His divine hand had brought health to the sick and life to the dying. The day had seemed to them like heaven on earth, and they were unconscious of how long it had been since they had eaten anything.

The sun was sinking in the west, and yet the people lingered. Finally the disciples came to Christ, urging that for their own sake the multitude should be sent away. Many had come from far and had eaten nothing since morning. In the surrounding towns and villages they might be able to obtain food. But Jesus said, "Give ye them to eat." Matthew 14:16. Then, turning to Philip, He questioned, "Whence shall we buy bread, that these may eat?" John 6:5.

Philip looked over the sea of heads and thought how impossible it would be to provide food for so great a company. He answered that two hundred pennyworth of bread would not be enough to divide among them so that each might have a little.

Jesus inquired how much food could be found among the company. "There is a lad here," said Andrew; "which hath five barley loaves, and two small fishes: but what are they among so many?" Verse 9. Jesus directed that these be brought to Him. Then He bade the disciples seat the people on the grass. When this was accomplished, He took the food, "and looking up to heaven, He blessed, and brake, and gave the loaves to His disciples, and the disciples to the multitude. And they did all eat, and were filled: and they took up of the fragments that remained twelve baskets full." Matthew 14:19, 20.

It was by a miracle of divine power that Christ fed the multitude; yet how humble was the fare provided–only the fishes and barley loaves that were the daily fare of the fisher-folk of Galilee.

Christ could have spread for the people a rich repast, but food prepared merely for the gratification of appetite would have conveyed no lesson for their good. Through this miracle Christ desired to teach a lesson of simplicity. If men today were simple in their habits, living in harmony with nature's laws, as did Adam and Eve in the beginning, there would be an abundant supply for the needs of the human family. But selfishness and the indulgence of appetite have brought sin and misery, from excess on the one hand, and from want on the other.

Jesus did not seek to attract the people to Him by gratifying the desire for luxury. To that great throng, weary and hungry after the long, exciting day, the simple fare was an assurance both of His power and of His tender care for them in the common needs of life. The Saviour has not promised His followers the luxuries of the world; their lot may be shut in by poverty; but His word is pledged that their need shall be supplied, and He has promised that which is better than earthly good—the abiding comfort of His own presence.

After the multitude had been fed, there was an abundance of food left. Jesus bade His disciples, "Gather up the fragments that remain, that nothing be lost." John 6:12. These words meant more than putting the food into baskets. The lesson was twofold. Nothing is to be wasted. We are to let slip no temporal advantage. We should neglect nothing that would serve to benefit a human being. Let everything be gathered up that will relieve the necessities of earth's hungry ones. With the same carefulness are we to treasure the bread from heaven to satisfy the needs of the soul. By every word of God we are to live. Nothing that God has spoken is to be lost. Not one word that concerns our eternal salvation are we to neglect. Not one word is to fall useless to the ground.

The miracle of the loaves teaches dependence upon God. When Christ fed the five thousand, the food was not nigh at hand. Apparently He had no means at His command. There He was, with five thousand men, besides women and children, in the wilderness. He had not invited the multitude to follow Him thither. Eager to be in His presence, they had come without invitation or command; but He knew that after listening all day to His instruction they were hungry and faint. They were far from home, and the night was at hand. Many of them were without means to purchase food. He who for their sake had fasted forty days in the wilderness, would not suffer them to return fasting to their homes.

The providence of God had placed Jesus where He was, and He depended on His heavenly Father for means to relieve the necessity. When we are brought into strait places, we are to depend on God. In every emergency we are to seek help from Him who has infinite resources at His command.

In this miracle, Christ received from the Father; He imparted to the disciples, the disciples to the people, and the people to one another. So all who are united to Christ will receive from Him the bread of life, and impart it to others. His disciples are the appointed means of communication between Christ and the people.

When the disciples heard the Saviour's direction, "Give ye them to eat," all the difficulties arose in their minds. They questioned, "Shall we go into the villages to buy food?" But what said Christ? "Give ye them to eat." The disciples brought to Jesus all they had; but He did not invite them to eat. He bade them serve the people. The food multiplied in His hands, and the hands of the disciples, reaching out to Christ, were never unfilled. The little store was sufficient for all. When the multitude had been fed, the disciples ate with Jesus of the precious, heaven-supplied food.

As we see the necessities of the poor, the ignorant, the afflicted, how often our hearts sink. We question, "What avail our feeble strength and slender resources to supply this terrible necessity? Shall we not wait for someone of greater ability to direct the work, or for some organization to undertake it?" Christ says, "Give ye them to eat." Use the means, the time, the ability, you have. Bring your barley loaves to Jesus.

Though your resources may not be sufficient to feed thousands, they may suffice to feed one. In the hand of Christ they may feed many. Like the disciples, give what you have. Christ will multiply the gift. He will reward honest, simple reliance upon Him. That which seemed but a meager supply will prove to be a rich feast.

See 2 Corinthians 9:6-11

THE TOUCH OF FAITH

"If I may but touch His garment, I shall be whole." Matthew 9:21. It was a poor woman who spoke these words–a woman who for twelve years had suffered from a disease that made her life a burden. She had spent all her means upon physicians and remedies, only to be pronounced incurable. But as she heard of the Great Healer, her hopes revived. She thought, "If only I could get near enough to speak to Him, I might be healed."

Christ was on His way to the home of Jairus, the Jewish rabbi who had entreated Him to come and heal his daughter. The heart-broken petition, "My little daughter lieth at the point of death: I pray Thee, come and lay Thy hands on her, that she may be healed" (Mark 5:23), had touched the tender, sympathetic heart of Christ, and He at once set out with the ruler for his home.

They advanced but slowly; for the crowd pressed Christ on every side. In making His way through the multitude, the Saviour came near to where the afflicted woman was standing. Again and again she had tried in vain to get near Him. Now her opportunity had come. She could see no way of speaking to Him. She would not seek to hinder His slow advance. But she had heard that healing came from a touch of His garments; and, fearful of losing her one chance for relief, she pressed forward, saying to herself, "If I may but touch His garment, I shall be whole."

Christ knew every thought of her mind, and He was making His way to where she stood. He realized her great need, and He was helping her to exercise faith.

As He was passing, she reached forward and succeeded in barely touching the border of His garment. That moment she knew that she was healed. In that one touch was concentrated the faith of her life, and instantly her pain and feebleness disappeared. Instantly she felt the thrill as of an electric current passing through every fiber of her being. There came over her a sensation of perfect health. "She felt in her body that she was healed of that plague." Verse 29.

The grateful woman desired to express her thanks to the Mighty Healer, who had done more for her in one touch than the physicians had done in twelve long years; but she dared not. With a grateful heart she tried to withdraw from the crowd. Suddenly Jesus stopped, and looking round He asked, "Who touched Me?"

Looking at Him in amazement, Peter answered, "Master, the multitude throng Thee and press Thee, and sayest Thou, Who touched Me?" Luke 8:45.

"Somebody hath touched Me," Jesus said; "for I perceive that virtue is gone out of Me." Verse 46. He could distinguish the touch of faith from the casual touch of the careless throng. Someone had touched Him with a deep purpose and had received answer.

Christ did not ask the question for His own information. He had a lesson for the people, for His disciples, and for the woman. He wished to inspire the afflicted with hope. He wished to show that it was faith which had brought the healing power. The woman's trust must not be passed by without comment. God must be glorified by her grateful confession. Christ desired her to understand that He approved her act of faith. He would not have her depart with a half blessing only. She was not to remain in ignorance of His knowledge of her suffering, or of His compassionate love and of His approval of her faith in His power to save to the uttermost all who come to Him.

Looking toward the woman, Christ insisted on knowing who had touched Him. Finding concealment vain, she came forward trembling, and cast herself at His feet. With grateful tears she told Him, before all the people, why she had touched His garment, and how she had been immediately healed. She feared that her act in touching His garment had been one of presumption; but no word of censure came from Christ's lips. He spoke only words of approval. They came from a heart of love, filled with sympathy for human woe. "Daughter," He said gently, "be of good comfort: thy faith hath made thee whole; go in peace." Verse 48. How cheering were these words to her. Now no fear that she had given offense embittered her joy.

To the curious crowd pressing about Jesus there was imparted no vital power. But the suffering woman who touched Him in faith received healing. So in spiritual things does the casual contact differ from the touch of faith. To believe in Christ merely as the Saviour of the world can never bring healing to the soul. The faith that is unto salvation is not a mere assent to the truth of the gospel. True faith is that which receives Christ as a personal Saviour. God gave His only-begotten Son, that I, by believing in Him, "should not perish, but have everlasting life." John 3:16. When I come to Christ, according to His word, I am to believe that I receive His saving grace. The life that I now live, I am to "live by the faith of the Son of God, who loved me, and gave Himself for me." Galatians 2:20.

Many hold faith as an opinion. Saving faith is a transaction, by which those who receive Christ join themselves in covenant relation with God. A living faith means an increase of vigor, a confiding trust, by which, through the grace of Christ, the soul becomes a conquering power.

Faith is a mightier conqueror than death. If the sick can be led to fix their eyes in faith upon the Mighty Healer, we shall see wonderful results. It will bring life to the body and to the soul.

In working for the victims of evil habits, instead of pointing them to the despair and ruin toward which they are hastening, turn their eyes away to Jesus. Fix them upon the glories of the heavenly. This will do more for the saving of body and soul than will all the terrors of the grave when kept before the helpless and apparently hopeless.

"Not by works of righteousness which we have done, but according to His mercy He saved us"

A centurion's servant was lying sick of the palsy. Among the Romans the servants were slaves, bought and sold in the market places, and often treated with abuse and cruelty; but the centurion was tenderly attached to his servant, and greatly desired his recovery. He believed that Jesus could heal him. He had not seen the Saviour, but the reports he had heard inspired him with faith. Notwithstanding the formalism of the Jews, this Roman was convinced that their religion was superior to his own. Already he had broken through the barriers of national prejudice and hatred that separated the conquerors from the conquered people. He had manifested respect for the service of God and had shown kindness to the Jews as His worshipers. In the teaching of Christ, as it had been reported to him, he found that which met the need of the soul. All that was spiritual within him responded to the Saviour's words. But he thought himself unworthy to approach Jesus, and he appealed to the Jewish elders to make request for his servant's healing.

The elders present the case to Jesus, urging that "he was worthy for whom He should do this: for he loveth our nation, and he hath built us a synagogue." Luke 7:4, 5.

But on the way to the centurion's home, Jesus receives a message from the officer himself, "Lord, trouble not Thyself: for I am not worthy that Thou shouldest enter under my roof." Verse 6.

Still the Saviour keeps on His way, and the centurion comes in person to complete the message, saying, "Neither thought I myself worthy to come unto Thee," "but speak the word only, and my servant shall be healed. For I am a man under authority, having soldiers under me: and I say to this man, Go, and he goeth; and to another, Come, and he cometh; and to my servant, Do this, and he doeth it." Verse 7; Matthew 8:8, 9.

"I represent the power of Rome, and my soldiers recognize my authority as supreme. So dost Thou represent the power of the infinite God, and all created things obey Thy word. Thou canst command the disease to depart, and it shall obey Thee. Speak but the word, and my servant shall be healed."

"As thou hast believed," Christ said, "so be it done unto thee. And his servant was healed in the selfsame hour." Verse 13.

The Jewish elders had commended the centurion to Christ because of the favor he had shown to "our nation." He is worthy, they said, for "he hath built us a synagogue." But the centurion said of himself, "I am not worthy." Yet he did not fear to ask help from Jesus. Not to his own goodness did he trust, but to the Saviour's mercy. His only argument was his great need.

In the same way every human being can come to Christ. "Not by works of righteousness which we have done, but according to His mercy He saved us." Titus 3:5. Do you feel that because you are a sinner you cannot hope to receive blessing from God? Remember that Christ came into the world to save sinners. We have nothing to recommend us to God; the plea that we may urge now and ever is our utterly helpless condition, which makes His redeeming power a necessity. Renouncing all self-dependence, we may look to the cross of Calvary and say:

"In my hand no price I bring;
Simply to Thy cross I cling."

"If thou canst believe, all things are possible to him that believeth." Mark 9:23. It is faith that connects us with heaven and brings us strength for coping with the powers of darkness. In Christ, God has provided means for subduing every evil trait and resisting every temptation, however strong. But many feel that they lack faith, and therefore they remain away from Christ. Let these souls, in their helpless unworthiness, cast themselves upon the mercy of their compassionate Saviour. Look not to self, but to Christ. He who healed the sick and cast out demons when He walked among men is still the same mighty Redeemer. Then grasp His promises as leaves from the tree of life: "Him that cometh to Me I will in no wise cast out." John 6:37. As you come to Him, believe that He accepts you, because He has promised. You can never perish while you do this–never.

"God commendeth His love toward us, in that, while we were yet sinners, Christ died for us." Romans 5:8.

And "if God be for us, who can be against us? He that spared not His own Son, but delivered Him up for us all, how shall He not with Him also freely give us all things?" Romans 8:31,32.

"I am persuaded, that neither death, nor life, nor angels, nor principalities, nor things present, nor things to come, nor powers, nor height, nor depth, nor any other creation, shall be able to separate us from the love of God, which is in Christ Jesus our Lord." Verses 38, 39.

LEPROSY

Of all the diseases known in the East the leprosy was most dreaded. Its incurable and contagious character, and its horrible effect upon its victims, filled the bravest with fear. Among the Jews it was regarded as a judgment on account of sin, and hence was called "the stroke," "the finger of God." Deep-rooted, ineradicable, deadly, it was looked upon as a symbol of sin.

By the ritual law the leper was pronounced unclean. Whatever he touched was unclean. The air was polluted by his breath. Like one already dead, he was shut out from the habitations of men. One who was suspected of having the disease must present himself to the priests, who were to examine and decide his case. If pronounced a leper, he was isolated from his family, cut off from the congregation of Israel, and doomed to associate with those only who were similarly afflicted.

Even kings and rulers were not exempt. A monarch attacked by this terrible disease must yield up the scepter and flee from society.

Away from his friends and his kindred the leper must bear the curse of his malady. He was obliged to publish his own calamity, to rend his garments, and sound the alarm, warning all to flee from his contaminating presence. The cry, "Unclean! unclean!" coming in mournful tones from the lonely exile, was a signal heard with fear and abhorrence.

In the region of Christ's ministry were many of these sufferers, and as the news of His work reached them, there is one in whose heart faith begins to spring up. If he could go to Jesus he might be healed. But how can he find Jesus? Doomed as he is to perpetual isolation, how can he present himself to the Healer? And will Christ heal him? Will He not, like the Pharisees, and even the physicians pronounce a curse upon him and warn him to flee from the haunts of men?

He thinks of all that has been told him of Jesus. Not one who has sought His help has been turned away. The wretched man determines to find the Saviour. Though shut out from the cities, it may be that he can cross His path in some byway along the mountain roads, or find Him as He is teaching outside the towns. The difficulties are great, but this is his only hope.

Standing afar off, the leper catches a few words from the Saviour's lips. He sees Him laying His hands upon the sick. He sees the lame, the blind, the paralytic, and those dying of various maladies rise up in health, praising God for deliverance. His faith strengthens. Nearer and yet nearer he approaches to the listening throng. The restrictions laid upon him, the safety of the people, the fear with which all men regard him, are alike forgotten. He thinks only of the blessed hope of healing.

He is a loathsome spectacle. The disease has made frightful inroads, and his decaying body is horrible to look upon. At sight of him the people fall back. In their terror they crowd upon one another to escape from contact with him. Some try to prevent him from approaching Jesus, but in vain. He neither sees nor hears them. Their expressions of loathing are lost upon him. He sees only the Son of God, he hears only the voice that speaks life to the dying.

Pressing to Jesus, he casts himself at His feet with the cry, "Lord, if Thou wilt, Thou canst make me clean."

Jesus replies, "I will; be thou clean," and lays His hand upon him. Matthew 8:2, 3.

Immediately a change passes over the leper. His blood becomes healthy, the nerves sensitive, the muscles firm. The unnaturally white, scaly surface peculiar to leprosy disappears; and his flesh becomes as the flesh of a little child.

Should the priests learn the facts concerning the healing of the leper, their hatred of Christ might lead them to render a dishonest sentence. Jesus desired that an impartial decision be secured. He therefore bids the man tell no one of the cure, but without delay present himself at the temple with an offering before any rumors concerning the miracle should be spread abroad. Before the priests could accept such an offering, they were required to examine the offerer and certify his complete recovery.

This examination was made. The priests who had condemned the leper to banishment testified to his cure. The healed man was restored to his home and society. He felt that the boon of health was very precious. He rejoiced in the vigor of manhood and in his restoration to his family. Notwithstanding the caution of Jesus, he could no longer conceal the fact of his cure, and joyfully he went about proclaiming the power of the One who had made him whole.

When this man came to Jesus, he was "full of leprosy," Its deadly poison permeated his whole body. The disciples sought to prevent their Master from touching him; for he who touched a leper became himself unclean. But in laying His hand upon the leper, Jesus received no defilement. The leprosy was cleansed. Thus it is with the leprosy of sin-deep-rooted, deadly, impossible to be cleansed by human power. "The whole head is sick, and the whole heart faint. From the sole of the foot even unto the head there is no soundness in it; but wounds, and bruises, and putrefying sores." Isaiah 1:5, 6. But Jesus, coming to dwell in humanity, receives no pollution. His presence was healing virtue for the sinner. Whoever will fall at His feet, saying in faith, "Lord, if Thou wilt, Thou canst make me clean," shall hear the answer, "I will; be thou clean."

In some instances of healing, Jesus did not at once grant the blessing sought. But in the case of leprosy no sooner was the appeal made than it was granted. When we pray for earthly blessings, the answer to our prayer may be delayed, or God may give us something other than we ask; but not so when we ask for deliverance from sin. It is His will to cleanse us from sin, to make us His children, and to enable us to live a holy life. Christ "gave Himself for our sins, that He might deliver us from this present evil world, according to the will of God and our Father." Galatians 1:4. "And this is the confidence that we have in Him, that, if we ask anything according to His will, He heareth us: and if we know that He hear us, whatsoever we ask, we know that we have the petitions that we desired of him." 1 John 5:14, 15.

Jesus looked upon the distressed and heart-burdened those whose hopes were blighted, and who with earthly joys were seeking to quiet the longing of the soul, and He invited all to find rest in Him.

"YE SHALL FIND REST."

Tenderly He bade the toiling people, "Take My yoke upon you, and learn of Me; for I am meek and lowly in heart: and ye shall find rest unto your souls." Matthew 11:29. In these words, Christ was speaking to every human being. Whether they know it or not, all are weary and heavy-laden. All are weighed down with burdens that only Christ can remove. The heaviest burden that we bear is the burden of sin. If we were left to bear this burden, it would crush us. But the Sinless One has taken our place. "The Lord hath laid on Him the iniquity of us all." Isaiah 53:6.

He has borne the burden of our guilt. He will take the load from our weary shoulders. He will give us rest. The burden of care and sorrow also He will bear. He invites us to cast all our care upon Him; for He carries us upon His heart.

The Elder Brother of our race is by the eternal throne. He looks upon every soul who is turning his face toward Him as the Saviour. He knows by experience what are the weaknesses of humanity, what are our wants, and where lies the strength of our temptations; for He was "in all points tempted like as we are, yet without sin." Hebrews 4:15. He is watching over you, trembling child of God. Are you tempted? He will deliver. Are you weak? He will strengthen. Are you ignorant? He will enlighten. Are you wounded? He will heal. The Lord "telleth the number of the stars;" and yet "He healeth the broken in heart, and bindeth up their wounds." Psalm 147:4, 3.

Whatever your anxieties and trials, spread out your case before the Lord. Your spirit will be braced for endurance. The way will be open for you to disentangle yourself from embarrassment and difficulty. The weaker and more helpless you know yourself to be, the stronger will you become in His strength. The heavier your burdens, the more blessed the rest in casting them upon your Burden Bearer.

Circumstances may separate friends; the restless waters of the wide sea may roll between us and them. But no circumstances, no distance, can separate us from the Saviour. Wherever we may be, He is at our right hand, to support, maintain, uphold, and cheer. Greater than the love of a mother for her child is Christ's love for His redeemed. It is our privilege to rest in His love, to say, "I will trust Him; for He gave His life for me."

Human love may change, but Christ's love knows no change. When we cry to Him for help, His hand is stretched out to save.

"The mountains may depart,
And the hills be removed;
But My loving-kindness shall not depart from thee, Neither shall My covenant of peace be removed, Saith Jehovah that hath mercy on thee." Isaiah 54:10, A.R.V.

HEALING OF THE SOUL

Many of those who came to Christ for help had brought disease upon themselves, yet He did not refuse to heal them. And when virtue from Him entered into these souls, they were convicted of sin, and many were healed of their spiritual disease as well as of their physical maladies.

Among these was the paralytic at Capernaum. Like the leper, this paralytic had lost all hope of recovery. His disease was the result of a sinful life, and his sufferings were embittered by remorse. In vain he had appealed to the Pharisees and doctors for relief; they pronounced him incurable, they denounced him as a sinner and declared that he would die under the wrath of God.

The palsied man had sunk into despair. Then he heard of the works of Jesus. Others, as sinful and helpless as he, had been healed, and he was encouraged to believe that he, too, might be cured if he could be carried to the Saviour. But hope fell as he remembered the cause of his malady, yet he could not cast away the possibility of healing.

His great desire was relief from the burden of sin. He longed to see Jesus and receive the assurance of forgiveness and peace with heaven. Then he would be content to live or to die, according to God's will.

There was no time to lose; already his wasted flesh bore signs of death. He besought his friends to carry him on his bed to Jesus, and this they gladly undertook to do. But so dense was the crowd that had assembled in and about the house where the Saviour was, that it was impossible for the sick man and his friends to reach Him, or even to come within hearing of His voice. Jesus was teaching in the home of Peter. According to their custom, His disciples sat close about Him, and "there were Pharisees and doctors of the law sitting by, who were come out of every village of Galilee and Judea and Jerusalem." Luke 5:17, A.R.V. Many of these had come as spies, seeking an accusation against Jesus. Beyond these thronged the promiscuous multitude, the eager, the reverent, the curious, and the unbelieving. Different nationalities and all grades of society were represented. "And the power of the Lord was present to heal." Verse 17. The Spirit of life brooded over the assembly, but Pharisees and doctors did not discern His presence. They felt no sense of need, and the healing was not for them. "He hath filled the hungry with good things; and the rich He hath sent empty away." Luke 1:53.

Again and again the bearers of the paralytic tried to push their way through the crowd, but in vain. The sick man looked about him in unutterable anguish. How could he relinquish hope when the longed-for help was so near? At his suggestion his friends bore him to the top of the house and, breaking up the roof, let him down at the feet of Jesus.

The discourse was interrupted. The Saviour looked upon the mournful countenance and saw the pleading eyes fixed upon Him. Well He knew the longing of that burdened soul. It was Christ who had brought conviction to his conscience when he was yet at home. When he repented of his sins and believed in the power of Jesus to make him whole, the mercy of the Saviour had blessed his heart. Jesus had watched the first glimmer of faith grow into a conviction that He was the sinner's only helper, and had seen it grow stronger with every effort to come into His presence. It was Christ who had drawn the sufferer to Himself. Now, in words that fell like music on the listener's ear, the Saviour said, "Son, be of good cheer; thy sins be forgiven thee." Matthew 9:2.

The burden of guilt rolls from the sick man's soul. He cannot doubt. Christ's words reveal His power to read the heart.

Who can deny His power to forgive sins? Hope takes the place of despair, and joy of oppressive gloom. The man's physical pain is gone, and his whole being is transformed. Making no further request, he lay in peaceful silence, too happy for words.

Many were watching with breathless interest every movement in this strange transaction. Many felt that Christ's words were an invitation to them. Were they not soul-sick because of sin? Were they not anxious to be freed from this burden?

But the Pharisees, fearful of losing their influence with the multitude, said in their hearts, "He blasphemeth: who can forgive sins but One, even God?" Mark 2:7, R.V.

Fixing His glance upon them, beneath which they cowered and

drew back, Jesus said, "Wherefore think ye evil in your hearts? For whether is easier, to say, Thy sins be forgiven thee; or to say, Arise, and walk? But that ye may know that the Son of man hath power on earth to forgive sins," He said, turning to the paralytic, "Arise, take up thy bed, and go unto thine house." Matthew 9:4-6.

Then he who had been borne on a litter to Jesus rose to his feet with the elasticity and strength of youth. And immediately he "took up the bed, and went forth before them all; insomuch that they were all amazed, and glorified God, saying, We never saw it on this fashion." Mark 2:12.

It required nothing less than creative power to restore health to that decaying body. The same voice that spoke life to man created from the dust of the earth, had spoken life to the dying paralytic. And the same power that gave life to the body had renewed the heart. He who at creation "spake, and it was," who "commanded, and it stood fast" (Psalm 33:9), had spoken life to the soul dead in trespasses and sins. The healing of the body was an evidence of the power that had renewed the heart. Christ bade the paralytic arise and walk, "that ye may know," He said, "that the Son of man hath power on earth to forgive sins."

The paralytic found in Christ healing for both the soul and the body. He needed health of soul before he could appreciate health of body. Before the physical malady could be healed, Christ must bring relief to the mind, and cleanse the soul from sin. This lesson should not be overlooked. There are today thousands suffering from physical disease who, like the paralytic, are longing for the message, "Thy sins are forgiven." The burden of sin, with its unrest and unsatisfied desires, is the foundation of their maladies. They can find no relief until they come to the Healer of the soul. The peace which He alone can impart would restore vigor to the mind and health to the body.

The effect produced upon the people by the healing of the paralytic was as if heaven had opened and revealed the glories of the better world. As the man who had been cured passed through the throng, blessing God at every step and bearing his burden as if it were a feather's weight, the people fell back to give him room and with awe-stricken faces gazed upon him, whispering softly among themselves, "We have seen strange things today." Luke 5:26.

In the home of the paralytic there was great rejoicing when he returned to his family, carrying with ease the couch upon which he had been slowly borne from their presence but a short time before. They gathered round with tears of joy, hardly daring to believe their eyes. He stood before them in the full vigor of manhood. Those arms that they had seen lifeless were quick to obey his will. The flesh that had been shrunken and leaden-hued was now fresh and ruddy. He walked with a firm, free step. Joy and hope were written in every lineament of his countenance, and an expression of purity and peace had taken the place of the marks of sin and suffering. Glad thanksgiving went up from that home, and God was glorified through His Son, who had restored hope to the hopeless and strength to the stricken one. This man and his family were ready to lay down their lives for Jesus. No doubt dimmed their faith, no unbelief marred their fealty to Him who had brought light into their darkened home. See Psalm 103:1-14.

"WILT THOU BE MADE WHOLE?"

"Now there is at Jerusalem by the sheep market a pool, which is called in the Hebrew tongue Bethesda, having five porches. In these lay a great multitude of impotent folk, of blind, halt, withered, waiting for the moving of the water." John 5:2, 3.

At certain seasons the waters of this pool were agitated, and it was commonly believed that this was the result of supernatural power, and that whoever first after the troubling of the pool stepped into the waters, would be healed of whatever disease he might have. Hundreds of sufferers visited the place; but so great was the crowd when the water was troubled that they rushed forward, trampling, underfoot men, women, and children, weaker than themselves. Many could not get near the pool. Many who had succeeded in reaching it died upon its bank. Shelters had been erected about the place, that the sick might be protected from the heat by the day and the chilliness of the night. There were some who spent the night in these porches, creeping to the edge of the pool day after day, in the vain hope of relief. Jesus was at Jerusalem. Walking alone in apparent meditation and prayer, He came to the pool. He saw the wretched sufferers watching for that which they supposed to be their only chance of cure. He longed to exercise His healing power and make every sufferer whole. But it was the Sabbath day. Multitudes were going to the temple for worship, and He knew that such an act of healing would so excite the prejudice of the Jews as to cut short His work.

But the Saviour saw one case of supreme wretchedness. It was that of a man who had been a helpless cripple for thirty-eight years. His disease was in a great degree the result of his own evil habits and was looked upon as a judgment from God. Alone and friendless, feeling that he was shut out from God's mercy, the sufferer had passed long years of misery. At the time when it was expected that the water would be troubled, those who pitied his helplessness would bear him to the porches. But at the favored moment he had no one to help him in. He had seen the rippling of the water, but had never been able to get farther than the edge of the pool. Others stronger than he would plunge in before him. The poor, helpless sufferer was unable to contend successfully with the scrambling, selfish crowd. His persistent efforts toward the one object, and his anxiety and continual disappointment, were fast wearing away the remnant of his strength.

The sick man was lying on his mat and occasionally lifting his head to gaze at the pool, when a tender, compassionate face bent over him, and the words, "Wilt thou be made whole?" arrested his attention. Hope came to his heart. He felt that in some way he was to have help. But the glow of encouragement soon faded. He remembered how often he had tried to reach the pool, and now he had little prospect of living till it should again be troubled. He turned away wearily, saying, "Sir, I have no man, when the water is troubled, to put me into the pool: but while I am coming, another steppeth down before me."

Jesus bids him, "Rise, take up thy bed, and walk." Verses 6-8. With a new hope the sick man looks upon Jesus. The expression of His countenance, the tones of His voice, are like no other. Love and power seem to breathe from His very presence. The cripple's faith takes hold upon Christ's word. Without question he sets his will to obey, and, as he does this, his whole body responds.

Every nerve and muscle thrills with new life, and healthful action comes to his crippled limbs. Springing to his feet, he goes on his way with firm, free step, praising God and rejoicing in his new-found strength.

Jesus had given the palsied man no assurance of divine help. The man might have said, "Lord, if Thou wilt make me whole, I will obey Thy word." He might have stopped to doubt, and thus have lost his one chance of healing. But no, he believed Christ's word, believed that he was made whole; immediately he made the effort, and God gave him the power; he willed to walk, and he did walk. Acting on the word of Christ, he was made whole.

By sin we have been severed from the life of God. Our souls are palsied. Of ourselves we are no more capable of living a holy life than was the impotent man capable of walking. Many realize their helplessness; they are longing for that spiritual life which will bring them into harmony with God, and are striving to obtain it. But in vain. In despair they cry, "O wretched man that I am! who shall deliver me from this body of death?" Romans 7:24, margin. Let these desponding, struggling ones look up. The Saviour is bending over the purchase of His blood, saying with inexpressible tenderness and pity, "Wilt thou be made whole?" He bids you arise in health and peace. Do not wait to feel that you are made whole. Believe the Saviour's word. Put your will on the side of Christ. Will to serve Him, and in acting upon His word you will receive strength. Whatever may be the evil practice, the master passion which through long indulgence binds both soul and body, Christ is able and longs to deliver. He will impart life to the soul that is "dead in trespasses." Ephesians 2:1. He will set free the captive that is held by weakness and misfortune and the chains of sin.

The sense of sin has poisoned the springs of life. But Christ says, "I will take your sins; I will give you peace. I have bought you with My blood. You are Mine. My grace shall strengthen your weakened will; your remorse for sin I will remove." When temptations assail you, when care and perplexity surround you, when, depressed and discouraged, you are ready to yield to despair, look to Jesus, and the darkness that encompasses you will be dispelled by the bright shining of His presence. When sin struggles for the mastery in your soul, and burdens the conscience, look to the Saviour. His grace is sufficient to subdue sin. Let your grateful heart, trembling with uncertainty, turn to Him. Lay hold on the hope set before you. Christ waits to adopt you into His family. His strength will help your weakness; He will lead you step by step. Place your hand in His, and let Him guide you.

Never feel that Christ is far away. He is always near. His loving presence surrounds you. Seek Him as One who desires to be found of you. He desires you not only to touch His garments, but to walk with Him in constant communion.

"GO, AND SIN NO MORE."

The Feast of Tabernacles had just ended. The priests and rabbis at Jerusalem had been defeated in their plottings against Jesus, and, as evening fell, "every man went unto his own house. Jesus went unto the Mount of Olives." John 7:53; 8:1.

From the excitement and confusion of the city, from the eager crowds and the treacherous rabbis, Jesus turned away to the quiet of the olive groves, where He could be alone with God. But in the early morning He returned to the temple; and as the people gathered about Him, He sat down and taught them.

He was soon interrupted. A group of Pharisees and scribes approached Him, dragging with them a terror-stricken woman, whom with hard, eager voices they accused of having violated the seventh commandment. Pushing her into the presence of Jesus, they said, with a hypocritical display of respect, "Master, this woman was taken in adultery, in the very act. Now Moses in the law commanded us, that such should be stoned: but what sayest Thou? Verses 4, 5. Their pretended reverence veiled a deep-laid plot for His ruin. Should Jesus acquit the woman, He might be charged with despising the law of Moses. Should He declare her worthy of death, He could be accused to the Romans as one who assumed authority belonging only to them.

Jesus looked upon the scene–the trembling victim in her shame, the hard-faced dignitaries, devoid of even human pity. His spirit of stainless purity shrank from the spectacle. Giving no sign that He had heard the question, He stooped and, fixing His eyes upon the ground, began to write in the dust.

Impatient at His delay and apparent indifference the accusers drew nearer, urging the matter upon His attention. But as their eyes, following those of Jesus, fell upon the pavement at His feet, their voices were silenced. There, traced before them, were the guilty secrets of their own lives.

Rising, and fixing His eyes upon the plotting elders, Jesus said, "He that is without sin among you, let him first cast a stone at her." Verse 7. And, stooping down, He continued writing.

He had not set aside the Mosaic law nor infringed upon the authority of Rome. The accusers were defeated. Now, their robes of pretended holiness torn from them, they stood, guilty and condemned, in the presence of infinite purity. Trembling lest the hidden iniquity of their lives should be laid open to the multitude, with bowed heads and downcast eyes they stole away, leaving their victim with the pitying Saviour.

Jesus arose and, looking upon the woman, said, "Where are those thine accusers? hath no man condemned thee? She said, No man, Lord. And Jesus said unto her, Neither do I condemn thee: go, and sin no more." Verses 10, 11.

The woman had stood before Jesus, cowering with fear. His words, "He that is without sin among you, let him first cast a stone," had come to her as a death sentence. She dared not lift her eyes to the Saviour's face, but silently awaited her doom. In astonishment she saw her accusers depart speechless and confounded; then those words of hope fell upon her ear, "Neither do I condemn thee: go, and sin no more." Her heart was melted, and, casting herself at the feet of Jesus, she sobbed out her grateful love and with bitter tears confessed her sins.

This was to her the beginning of a new life, a life of purity and peace, devoted to God. In the uplifting of this fallen soul, Jesus performed a greater miracle than in healing the most grievous physical disease; He cured the spiritual malady which is unto death everlasting. This penitent woman became one of His most steadfast followers. With self-sacrificing love and devotion she showed her gratitude for His forgiving mercy. For this erring woman the world had only contempt and scorn, but the Sinless One pitied her weakness and reached to her a helping hand. While the hypocritical Pharisees denounced, Jesus bade her, "Go, and sin no more."

Jesus knows the circumstances of every soul. The greater the sinner's guilt, the more he needs the Saviour. His heart of divine love and sympathy is drawn out most of all for the one who is the most hopelessly entangled in the snares of the enemy. With His own blood

He has signed the emancipation papers of the race.

Jesus does not desire those who have been purchased at such a cost to become the sport of the enemy's temptations. He does not desire us to be overcome and perish. He who curbed the lions in their den, and walked with His faithful witnesses amid the fiery flames, is just as ready to work in our behalf to subdue every evil in our nature. Today He is standing at the altar of mercy, presenting before God the prayers of those who desire His help. He turns no weeping, contrite one away. Freely will He pardon all who come to Him for forgiveness and restoration. He does not tell to any all that He might reveal, but He bids every trembling soul take courage. Whosoever will, may take hold of God's strength, and make peace with Him, and He will make peace.

The souls that turn to Him for refuge, Jesus lifts above the accusing and the strife of tongues. No man or evil angel can impeach these souls. Christ unites them to His own divine-human nature. They stand besides the great Sin Bearer in the light proceeding from the throne of God.

The blood of Jesus Christ cleanses "from all sin." 1 John 1:7.

"Who shall lay anything to the charge of God's elect? It is God that justifieth. Who is he that condemneth? It is Christ that died, yea rather, that is risen again, who is even at the right hand of God, who also maketh intercession for us." Romans 8:33, 34.

Over the winds and the waves, and over men possessed of demons, Christ showed that He had absolute control. He who stilled the tempest and calmed the troubled sea spoke peace to minds distracted and overborne by Satan.

In the synagogue at Capernaum, Jesus was speaking of His mission to set free the slaves of sin. He was interrupted by a shriek of terror. A madman rushed forward from among the people, crying out, "Let us alone; what have we to do with Thee, Thou Jesus of Nazareth? art Thou come to destroy us? I know Thee who Thou art, the Holy One of God." Mark 1:24.

Jesus rebuked the demon, saying, "Hold thy peace, and come out of him. And when the devil had thrown him in the midst, he came out of him, and hurt him not." Luke 4:35.

The cause of this man's affliction also was in his own life. He had been fascinated with the pleasures of sin and had thought to make life a grand carnival. Intemperance and frivolity perverted the noble attributes of his nature, and Satan took entire control of him. Remorse came too late. When he would have sacrificed wealth and pleasure to regain his lost manhood he had become helpless in the grasp of the evil one.

In the Saviour's presence he was roused to long for freedom, but the demon resisted the power of Christ. When the man tried to appeal to Jesus for help, the evil spirit put words into his mouth, and he cried out in an agony of fear. The demoniac partially comprehended that he was in the presence of One who could set him free; but when he tried to come within reach of that mighty hand, another's will held him, another's words found utterance through him.

The conflict between the power of Satan and his own desire for freedom was terrible. It seemed that the tortured man must lose his life in the struggle with the foe that had been the ruin of his manhood. But the Saviour spoke with authority and set the captive free. The man who had been possessed stood before the wondering people in the freedom of self-possession. With glad voice he praised God for deliverance. The eye that had so lately glared with the fire of insanity now beamed with intelligence and overflowed with grateful tears. The people were dumb with amazement. As soon as they recovered speech they exclaimed one to another, "What is this? a new teaching! with authority He commandeth even the unclean spirits, and they obey Him." Mark 1:27, R.V.

There are multitudes today as truly under the power of evil spirits as was the demoniac of Capernaum. All who willfully depart from God's commandments are placing themselves under the control of Satan. Many a man tampers with evil, thinking that he can break away at pleasure; but he is lured on and on, until he finds himself controlled by a will stronger than his own. He cannot escape its mysterious power. Secret sin or master passion may hold him a captive as helpless as was the demoniac of Capernaum.

Yet his condition is not hopeless. God does not control our minds without our consent; but every man is free to choose what power he will have to rule over him. None have fallen so low, none are so vile, but that they may find deliverance in Christ. The demoniac, in place of prayer, could utter only the words of Satan; yet the heart's unspoken appeal was heard. No cry from a soul in need, though it fail of utterance in words, will be unheeded. Those who consent to enter into covenant with God are not left to the power of Satan or to the infirmity of their own nature.

"Shall the prey be taken from the mighty, or the lawful captive delivered? . . . Thus saith the Lord, Even the captives of the mighty shall be taken away, and the prey of the terrible shall be delivered: for I will contend with him that contendeth with thee, and I will save thy children." Isaiah 49:24, 25. Marvelous will be the transformation wrought in him who by faith opens the door of the heart to the Saviour.

"I GIVE UNTO YOU POWER."

Like the twelve apostles, the seventy disciples whom Christ sent forth later received supernatural endowments as a seal of their mission. When their work was completed, they returned with joy, saying, "Lord, even the devils are subject unto us through Thy name." Jesus answered, "I beheld Satan as lightning fall from heaven." Luke 10:17, 18.

Henceforth Christ's followers are to look upon Satan as a conquered foe. Upon the cross, Jesus was to gain the victory for them; that victory He desired them to accept as their own. "Behold," He said, "I give unto you power to tread on serpents and scorpions, and over all the power of the enemy: and nothing shall by any means hurt you." Verse 19.

The omnipotent power of the Holy Spirit is the defense of every contrite soul. No one who in penitence and faith has claimed His protection will Christ permit to pass under the enemy's power. It is true that Satan is a powerful being; but, thank God, we have a mighty Saviour, who cast out the evil one from heaven. Satan is pleased when we magnify his power. Why not talk of Jesus? Why not magnify His power and His love?

The rainbow of promise encircling the throne on high is an everlasting testimony that "God so loved the world, that He gave His only-begotten Son, that whosoever believeth in Him should not perish, but have everlasting life." John 3:16. It testifies to the universe that God will never forsake His children in the struggle with evil. It is an assurance to us of strength and protection as long as the throne itself shall endure.

THE CO-WORKING OF THE DIVINE AND THE HUMAN

In the ministry of healing the physician is to be a co-worker with Christ. The Saviour ministered to both the soul and the body. The gospel which He taught was a message of spiritual life and of physical restoration. Deliverance from sin and the healing of disease were linked together. The same ministry is committed to the Christian physician. He is to unite with Christ in relieving both the physical and spiritual needs of his fellow men. He is to be to the sick a messenger of mercy, bringing to them a remedy for the diseased body and for the sin-sick soul.

Christ is the true head of the medical profession. The chief Physician, He is at the side of every God-fearing practitioner who works to relieve human suffering. While the physician uses nature's remedies for physical disease, he should point his patients to Him who can relieve the maladies of both the soul and the body. That which physicians can only aid in doing, Christ accomplishes. They endeavor to assist nature's work of healing; Christ Himself is the healer. The physician seeks to preserve life; Christ imparts life.

THE SOURCE OF HEALING

The Saviour in His miracles revealed the power that is continually at work in man's behalf, to sustain and to heal him. Through the agencies of nature, God is working, day by day, hour by hour, moment by moment, to keep us alive, to build up and restore us. When any part of the body sustains injury, a healing process is at once begun; nature's agencies are set at work to restore soundness. But the power working through these agencies is the power of God. All life-giving power is from Him. When one recovers from disease, it is God who restores him.

Sickness, suffering, and death are work of an antagonistic power. Satan is the destroyer; God is the restorer.

The words spoken to Israel are true today of those who recover health of body or health of soul. "I am the Lord that healeth thee." Exodus 15:26.

The desire of God for every human being is expressed in the words, "Beloved, I wish above all things that thou mayest prosper and be in health, even as thy soul prospereth." 3 John 2. He it is who "forgiveth all thine iniquities; who healeth all thy diseases; who redeemeth thy life from destruction; who crowneth thee with loving-kindness and tender mercies." Psalm 103:3,4.

When Christ healed disease, He warned many of the afflicted ones, "Sin no more, lest a worse thing come unto thee." John 5:14. Thus He taught that they had brought disease upon themselves by transgressing the laws of God, and that health could be preserved only by obedience.

The physician should teach his patients that they are to cooperate with God in the work of restoration. The physician has a continually increasing realization of the fact that disease is the result of sin. He knows that the laws of nature, as truly as the precepts of the Decalogue, are divine, and that only in obedience to them can health be recovered or preserved. He sees many suffering as the result of hurtful practices who might be restored to health if they would do what they might for their own restoration. They need to be taught that every practice which destroys the physical, mental, or spiritual energies is sin, and that health is to be secured through obedience to the laws that God has established for the good of all mankind.

When a physician sees a patient suffering from disease caused by improper eating and drinking or other wrong habits, yet neglects to tell him of this, he is doing his fellow being an injury. Drunkards, maniacs, those who are given over to licentiousness, all appeal to the physician to declare clearly and distinctly that suffering results from sin. Those who understand the principles of life should be in earnest in striving to counteract the causes of disease. Seeing the continual conflict with pain, laboring constantly to alleviate suffering, how can the physician hold his peace? Is he benevolent and merciful if he does not teach strict temperance as a remedy for disease?

Let it be made plain that the way of God's commandments is the way of life. God has established the laws of nature, but His laws are not arbitrary exactions. Every "Thou shalt not," whether in physical or in moral law, implies a promise. If we obey it, blessing will attend our steps. God never forces us to do right, but He seeks to save us from the evil and lead us to the good.

Let attention be called to the laws that were taught to Israel. God gave them definite instruction in regard to their habits of life. He made known to them the laws relating to both physical and spiritual well-being; and on condition of obedience He assured them, "The Lord will take away from thee all sickness." Deuteronomy 7:15. "Set your hearts unto all the words which I testify among you this day." "For they are life unto those that find them, and health to all their flesh." Deuteronomy 32:46; Proverbs 4:22. God desires us to reach the standard of perfection made possible for us by the gift of Christ. He calls upon us to make our choice on the right side, to connect with heavenly agencies, to adopt principles that will restore in us the divine image. In His written word and in the great book of nature He has revealed of the principles of life. It is our work to obtain a knowledge of these principles, and by obedience to co-operate with Him in restoring health to the body as well as to the soul.

Men need to learn that the blessings of obedience, in their fullness, can be theirs only as they receive the grace of Christ. It is His grace that gives man power to obey the laws of God. It is this that enables him to break the bondage of evil habit. This is the only power that can make him and keep him steadfast in the right path.

When the gospel is received in its purity and power, it is a cure for the maladies that originated in sin. The Sun of Righteousness arises, "with healing in His wings." Malachi 4:2. Not all this world bestows can heal a broken heart, or impart peace of mind, or remove care, or banish disease. Fame, genius, talent–all are powerless to gladden the sorrowful heart or to restore the wasted life. The life of God in the soul is man's only hope.

The love which Christ diffuses through the whole being is a vitalizing power. Every vital part–the brain, the heart, the nerves–it touches with healing. By it the highest energies of the being are roused to activity. It frees the soul from the guilt and sorrow, the anxiety and care, that crush the life forces. With it come serenity and composure. It implants in the soul, joy that nothing earthly can destroy,–joy in the Holy Spirit,–health-giving, life-giving joy.

Our Saviour's words, "Come unto Me, . . . and I will give you rest" (Matthew 11:28), are a prescription for the healing of physical, mental, and spiritual ills. Though men have brought suffering upon themselves by their own wrongdoing, He regards them with pity. In Him they may find help. He will do great things for those who trust in Him.

Although for ages sin has been strengthening its hold on the human race, although through falsehood and artifice Satan has cast the black shadow of his interpretation upon the word of God, and has caused men to doubt His goodness; yet the Father's mercy and love have not ceased to flow earthward in rich currents. If human beings would open the windows of the soul heavenward, in appreciation of the divine gifts, a flood of healing virtue would pour in.

The physician who desires to be an acceptable co-worker with Christ will strive to become efficient in every feature of his work. He will study diligently, that he may be well qualified for the responsibilities of his profession, and will constantly endeavor to reach a higher standard, seeking for increased knowledge, greater skill, and deeper discernment. Every physician should realize that he who does weak, inefficient work is not only doing injury to the sick, but is also doing injustice to his fellow physicians. The physician who is satisfied with a low standard of skill and knowledge not only belittles the medical profession, but does dishonor to Christ, the Chief Physician.

Those who find that they are unfitted for medical work should choose some other employment. Those who are well adapted to care for the sick, but whose education and medical qualifications are limited, would do well to take up the humbler parts of the work, ministering faithfully as nurses. By patient service under skillful physicians they may be constantly learning, and by improving every opportunity to acquire knowledge they may in time become fully qualified for the work of a physician. Let the younger physicians, "as workers together with Him [the Chief Physician], . . . receive not the grace of God in vain, . . . giving no offense in anything, that the ministry [of the sick] be not blamed: but in all things approving ourselves as the ministers of God." 2 Corinthians 6:1-4.

God's Purpose for us is that we shall ever move upward. The true medical missionary physician will be an increasingly skillful practitioner. Talented Christian physicians, having superior professional ability, should be sought out and encouraged to engage in the service of God in places where they can educate and train others to become medical missionaries.

The Physician should gather to his soul the light of the word of God. He should make continual growth in grace. With him, religion is not to be merely one influence among others. It is to be an influence dominating all others. He is to act from high, holy motives-motives that are powerful because they proceed from the One who gave His life to furnish us with power to overcome evil.

If the physician faithfully and diligently strives to make himself efficient in his profession, if he consecrates himself to the service of Christ, and takes time to search his own heart, he will understand how to grasp the mysteries of his sacred calling. He may so discipline and educate himself that all within the sphere of his influence will see the excellence of the education and wisdom gained by the one who is connected with the God of wisdom and power.

In no place is a closer fellowship with Christ needed than in the work of the physician. He who would rightly perform the physician's duties must daily and hourly live a Christian life. The life of the patient is in the hands of the physician. One careless diagnosis, one wrong prescription, in a critical case, or one unskillful movement of the hand in an operation, even by so much as a hair's breadth, and a life may be sacrificed, a soul launched into eternity. How solemn the thought! How important that the physician shall be ever under the control of the divine Physician!

The Saviour is willing to help all who call upon Him for wisdom and clearness of thought. And who needs wisdom and clearness of thought more than does the physician, upon whose decisions so much depends? Let the one who is trying to prolong life look in faith to Christ to direct his every movement. The Saviour will give him tact and skill in dealing with difficult cases.

Wonderful are the opportunities given to the guardians of the sick. In all that is done for the restoration of the sick, let them understand that the physician is seeking to help them co-operate with God in combating disease. Lead them to feel that at every step taken in harmony with the laws of God, they may expect the aid of divine power.

The sick and suffering will have much more confidence in the physician who they are confident loves and fears God. They rely upon his words. They feel a sense of safety in the presence and administration of that physician.

Knowing the Lord Jesus, it is the privilege of the Christian practitioner by prayer to invite His presence in the sickroom. Before performing a critical operation, let the physician ask for the aid of the Great Physician. Let him assure the suffering one that God can bring him safely through the ordeal, that in all times of distress He is a sure refuge for those who trust in Him. The physician who cannot do this loses case after case that otherwise might have been saved. If he could speak words that would inspire faith in the sympathizing Saviour, who feels every throb of anguish, and could present the needs of the soul to Him in prayer, the crisis would oftener be safely passed.

Only He who reads the heart can know with what trembling and terror many patients consent to an operation under the surgeon's hand. They realize their peril. While they may have confidence in the physician's skill they know that it is not infallible. But as they see the physician bowed in prayer, asking help from God, they are inspired with confidence. Gratitude and trust open the heart to the healing power of God, the energies of the whole being are vitalized, and the life forces triumph.

To the physician also the Saviour's presence is an element of strength. Often the responsibilities and possibilities of his work bring dread upon the spirit. The feverishness of uncertainty and fear would make the hand unskillful. But the assurance that the divine Counselor is beside him, to guide and to sustain, imparts quietness and courage. The touch of Christ upon the physician's hand brings vitality, restfulness, confidence, and power.

When the crisis is safely passed, and success is apparent, let a few moments be spent with the patient in prayer. Give expression to your thankfulness for the life that has been spared. As words of gratitude flow from the patient to the physician, let the praise and thanksgiving be directed to God. Tell the patient his life has been spared because he was under the heavenly Physician's protection.

The physician who follows such a course is leading his patient to the One upon whom he is dependent for life, the One who can save to the uttermost all who come to Him.

Into the medical missionary work should be brought a deep yearning for souls. To the physician equally with the gospel minister is committed the highest trust ever committed to man. Whether he realizes it or not, every physician is entrusted with the cure of souls.

In their work of dealing with disease and death, physicians too often lose sight of the solemn realities of the future life. In their earnest effort to avert the peril of the body, they forget the peril of the soul. The one to whom they are ministering may be losing his hold on life. Its last opportunities are slipping from his grasp. This soul the physician must meet again at the judgment seat of Christ.

Often we miss the most precious blessings by neglecting to speak a word in season. If the golden opportunity is not watched for, it will be lost. At the bedside of the sick no word of creed or controversy should be spoken. Let the sufferer be pointed to the One who is willing to save all that come to Him in faith. Earnestly, tenderly strive to help the soul that is hovering between life and death.

The physician who knows that Christ is his personal Saviour, because he himself has been led to the Refuge, knows how to deal with the trembling, guilty, sin-sick souls who turn to him for help. He can respond to the inquiry, "What must I do to be saved?" He can tell the story of the Redeemer's love. He can speak from experience of the power of repentance and faith. In simple, earnest words he can present the soul's need to God in prayer and can encourage the sick one also to ask for and accept the mercy of the compassionate Saviour. As he thus ministers at the bedside of the sick, striving to speak words that will bring help and comfort, the Lord works with him and through him. As the mind of the sufferer is directed to the Saviour, the peace of Christ fills his heart, and the spiritual health that comes to him is used as the helping hand of God in restoring the health of the body.

In attending the sick, the physician will often find opportunity for ministering to the friends of the afflicted one. As they watch by the bed of suffering, feeling powerless to prevent one pang of anguish, their hearts are softened. Often grief concealed from others is expressed to the physician. Then is the opportunity to point these sorrowing ones to Him who has invited the weary and heavy-laden to come unto Him. Often prayer can be offered for and with them, presenting their needs to the Healer of all woes, the Soother of all sorrows.

GOD'S PROMISES

The physician has precious opportunities for directing his patients to the promises of God's word. He is to bring from the treasure house things new and old, speaking here and there the words of comfort and instruction that are longed for. Let the physician make his mind a storehouse of fresh thoughts. Let him study the word of God diligently, that he may be familiar with its promises. Let him learn to repeat the comforting words that Christ spoke during His earthly ministry when giving His lessons and healing the sick. He should talk of the works of healing wrought by Christ, of His tenderness and love. Never should he neglect to direct the minds of his patients to Christ, the Chief Physician.

The same power that Christ exercised when He walked visibly among men is in His word. It was by His word that Jesus healed disease and cast out demons; by His word He stilled the sea and raised the dead, and the people bore witness that His word was with power. He spoke the word of God, as He had spoken to all the prophets and teachers of the Old Testament. The whole Bible is a manifestation of Christ.

The Scriptures are to be received as God's word to us, not written merely, but spoken. When the afflicted ones came to Christ, He beheld not only those who asked for help, but all who throughout the ages should come to Him in like need and with like faith. When He said to the paralytic, "Son, be of good cheer; thy sins be forgiven thee;" when He said to the woman of Capernaum, "Daughter, be of good comfort: thy faith hath made thee whole; go in peace," He spoke to other afflicted, sin-burdened ones who should seek His help. Matthew 9:2; Luke 8:48.

So with all the promises of God's word. In them He is speaking to us individually, speaking as directly as if we could listen to His voice. It is in these promises that Christ communicates to us His grace and power. They are leaves from that tree which is "for the healing of the nations." Rev. 22:2. Received, assimilated, they are to be the strength of the character, the inspiration and sustenance of the life. Nothing else can have such healing power. Nothing besides can impart the courage and faith which give vital energy to the whole being.

To one who stands trembling with fear on the brink of the grave, to the soul weary of the burden of suffering and sin, let the physician as he has opportunity repeat the words of the Saviour–for all the words of Holy Writ are His: "Like as a father pitieth his children, so the Lord pitieth them that fear him." Psalm 103:13, 14.

"Only acknowledge thine iniquity, that thou hast transgressed against the Lord thy God, and hast scattered thy ways to the strangers under every green tree, and ye have not obeyed my voice, saith the Lord." Jeremiah 3:13.

"If we confess our sins, he is faithful and just to forgive us our sins, and to cleanse us from all unrighteousness." 1 John 1:9.

"Come now, and let us reason together, saith the Lord: though your sins be as scarlet, they shall be as white as snow; though they be red like crimson, they shall be as wool. If ye be willing and obedient, ye shall eat the good of the land." Isaiah 1:18, 19.

"I have loved thee with an everlasting love: therefore with loving-kindness have I drawn thee." "I hid My face from thee for a moment; but with everlasting kindness will I have mercy on thee." Jeremiah 31:3; Isaiah 54:8.

"Let not your heart be troubled." "Peace I leave with you, My peace I give unto you: not as the world giveth, give I unto you. Let not your heart be troubled, neither let it be afraid." John 14:1, 27.

"A man shall be as an hiding place from the wind, and a covert from the tempest; as rivers of water in a dry place, as the shadow of a great rock in a weary land." Isaiah 32:2. "when the poor and needy seek water, and there is none, and their tongue faileth for thirst, I the Lord will hear them, I the God of Israel will not forsake them." Isaiah 41:17.

"Thus saith the Lord that made thee": "I will pour water upon him that is thirsty, and floods upon the dry ground: I will pour My Spirit upon thy seed, and My blessing upon thine offspring." Isaiah 44:2, 3.

"Look unto Me, and be ye saved, all the ends of the earth." Isaiah 45:22.

"Himself took our infirmities, and bare our sicknesses." "He was wounded for our transgressions, He was bruised for our iniquities: the chastisement of our peace was upon Him; and with His stripes we are healed." Matthew 8:17; Isaiah 53:5.

THE PHYSICIAN, AN EDUCATOR

The true physician is an educator. He recognizes his responsibility, not only to the sick who are under his direct care, but also to the community in which he lives. He stands as a guardian of both physical and moral health. It is his endeavor not only to teach right methods for the treatment of the sick, but to encourage right habits of living, and to spread a knowledge of right principles.

NEED OF EDUCATION IN HEALTH PRINCIPLES

Education in health principles was never more needed than now. Notwithstanding the wonderful progress in so many lines relating to the comforts and conveniences of life, even to sanitary matters and to the treatment of disease, the decline in physical vigor and power of endurance is alarming. It demands the attention of all who have at heart the well-being of their fellow men.

Our artificial civilization is encouraging evils destructive of sound principles. Custom and fashion are at war with nature. The practices they enjoin, and the indulgences they foster, are steadily lessening both physical and mental strength, and bringing upon the race an intolerable burden. Intemperance and crime, disease and wretchedness, are everywhere.

Many transgress the laws of health through ignorance, and they need instruction. But the greater number know better than they do. They need to be impressed with the importance of making their knowledge a guide of life. The physician has many opportunities both of imparting a knowledge of health principles and of showing the importance of putting them in practice. By right instruction he can do much to correct evils that are working untold harm.

A practice that is laying the foundation of a vast amount of disease and of even more serious evils is the free use of poisonous drugs. When attacked by disease, many will not take the trouble to search out the cause of their illness. Their chief anxiety is to rid themselves of pain and inconvenience. So they resort to patent nostrums, of whose real properties they know little, or they apply to a physician for some remedy to counteract the result of their misdoing, but with no thought of making a change in their unhealthful habits. If immediate benefit is not realized, another medicine is tried, and then another. Thus the evil continues.

People need to be taught that drugs do not cure disease. It is true that they sometimes afford present relief, and the patient appears to recover as the result of their use; this is because nature has sufficient vital force to expel the poison and to correct the conditions that caused the disease. Health is recovered in spite of the drug. But in most cases the drug only changes the form and location of the disease. Often the effect of the poison seems to be overcome for a time, but the results remain in the system and work great harm at some later period.

By the use of poisonous drugs, many bring upon themselves lifelong illness, and many lives are lost that might be saved by the use of natural methods of healing. The poisons contained in many so-called remedies create habits and appetites that mean ruin to both soul and body. Many of the popular nostrums called patent medicines, and even some of the drugs dispensed by physicians, act a part in laying the foundation of the liquor habit, the opium habit, the morphine habit, that are so terrible a curse to society.

The only hope of better things is in the education of the people in right principles. Let physicians teach the people that restorative power is not in drugs, but in nature. Disease is an effort of nature to free the system from conditions that result from a violation of the laws of health. In case of sickness, the cause should be ascertained. Unhealthful conditions should be changed, wrong habits corrected. Then nature is to be assisted in her effort to expel impurities and to re-establish right conditions in the system.

NATURAL REMEDIES

Pure air, sunlight, abstemiousness, rest, exercise, proper diet, the use of water, trust in divine power–these are the true remedies. Every person should have a knowledge of nature's remedial agencies and how to apply them. It is essential both to understand the principles involved in the treatment of the sick and to have a practical training that will enable one rightly to use this knowledge.

The use of natural remedies requires an amount of care and effort that many are not willing to give. Nature's process of healing and upbuilding is gradual, and to the impatient it seems slow. The surrender of hurtful indulgences requires sacrifice. But in the end it will be found that nature, untrammeled, does her work wisely and well. Those who persevere in obedience to her laws will reap the reward in health of body and health of mind.

Too little attention is generally given to the preservation of health. It is far better to prevent disease than to know how to treat it when contracted.

It is the duty of every person, for his own sake, and for the sake of humanity, to inform himself in regard to the laws of life and conscientiously to obey them. All need to become acquainted with that most wonderful of all organisms, the human body. They should understand the functions of the various organs and the dependence of one upon another for the healthy action of all. They should study the influence of the mind upon the body, and of the body upon the mind, and the laws by which they are governed.

TRAINING FOR LIFE'S CONFLICT

We cannot be too often reminded that health does not depend on chance. It is a result of obedience to law. This is recognized by the contestants in athletic games and trials of strength. These men make the most careful preparation. They submit to thorough training and strict discipline. Every physical habit is carefully regulated. They know that neglect, excess, or carelessness, which weakens or cripples any organ or function of the body, would ensure defeat.

How much more important is such carefulness to ensure success in the conflict of life. It is not mimic battles in which we are engaged. We are waging a warfare upon which hang eternal results. We have unseen enemies to meet. Evil angels are striving for the dominion of every human being. Whatever injures the health, not only lessens physical vigor, but tends to weaken the mental and moral powers. Indulgence in any unhealthful practice makes it more difficult for one to discriminate between right and wrong, and hence more difficult to resist evil. It increases the danger of failure and defeat.

"They which run in a race run all, but one receiveth the prize." 1 Corinthians 9:24. In the warfare in which we are engaged, all may win who will discipline themselves by obedience to right principles.

The practice of these principles in the details of life is too often looked upon as unimportant –a matter too trivial to demand attention. But in view of the issues at stake, nothing with which we have to do is small. Every act casts its weight into the scale that determines life's victory or defeat. The scriptures bids us, "So run, that ye may obtain." Verse 24.

With our first parents, intemperate desire resulted in the loss of Eden. Temperance in all things has more to do with our restoration to Eden than men realize.

Pointing to the self-denial practiced by the contestants in the ancient Greek games, the apostle Paul writes: "Every man that striveth for the mastery is temperate in all things. Now they do it to obtain a corruptible crown; but we an incorruptible. I therefore so run, not as uncertainly; so fight I, not as one that beateth the air: but I keep under my body, and bring it into subjection: lest that by any means, when I have preached to others, I myself should be a castaway." Verses 25-27. The progress of reform depends upon a clear recognition of fundamental truth. While, on the one hand, danger lurks in a narrow philosophy and a hard, cold orthodoxy, on the other hand there is great danger in a careless liberalism. The foundation of all enduring reform is the law of God. We are to present in clear, distinct lines the need of obeying this law. Its principles must be kept before the people. They are as everlasting and inexorable as God Himself.

One of the most deplorable effects of the original apostasy was the loss of man's power of self-control. Only as this power is regained can there be real progress.

The body is the only medium through which the mind and the soul are developed for the upbuilding of character. Hence it is that the adversary of souls directs his temptations to the enfeebling and degrading of the physical powers. His success here means the surrender to evil of the whole being. The tendencies of our physical nature, unless under the dominion of a higher power, will surely work ruin and death.

The body is to be brought into subjection. The higher powers of the being are to rule. The passions are to be controlled by the will, which is itself to be under the control of God. The kingly power of reason, sanctified by divine grace, is to bear sway in our lives.

The requirements of God must be brought home to the

conscience. Men and women must be awakened to the duty of self-mastery, the need of purity, freedom from every depraving appetite and defiling habit. They need to be impressed with the fact that all their powers of mind and body are the gift of God, and are to be preserved in the best possible condition for His service.

In that ancient ritual which was the gospel in symbol, no blemished offering could be brought to God's altar. The sacrifice that was to represent Christ must be spotless. The word of God points to this as an illustration of what His children are to be–"a living sacrifice," "holy and without blemish," "well-pleasing to God." Romans 12:I, R.V., margin; Ephesians 5:27.

Apart from divine power, no genuine reform can be effected. Human barriers against natural and cultivated tendencies are but as the sandbank against the torrent. Not until the life of Christ becomes a vitalizing power in our lives can we resist the temptations that assail us from within and from without.

Christ came to this world and lived the law of God, that man might have perfect mastery over the natural inclinations which corrupt the soul. The Physician of soul and body, He gives victory over warring lusts. He has provided every facility, that man may possess completeness of character.

When one surrenders to Christ, the mind is brought under the control of the law; but it is the royal law, which proclaims liberty to every captive. By becoming one with Christ, man is made free. Subjection to the will of Christ means restoration to perfect manhood.

Obedience to God is liberty from the thralldom of sin, deliverance from human passion and impulse. Man may stand conqueror of himself, conqueror of his own inclinations, conqueror of principalities and powers, and of "the rulers of the darkness of this world," and of "spiritual wickedness in high places." Ephesians 6:12.

In no place is such instruction as this more needed, and nowhere will it be productive of greater good, than in the home. Parents have to do with the very foundation of habit and character. The reformatory movement must begin in presenting to them the principles of the law of God as bearing upon both physical and moral health. Show that obedience to God's word is our only safeguard against the evils that are sweeping the world to destruction. Make plain the responsibility of parents, not only for themselves, but for their children. They are giving to their children an example either of obedience or of transgression. By their example and teaching, the destiny of their households is decided. The children will be what their parents make them.

If parents could be led to trace the result of their action, and could see how, by their example and teaching, they perpetuate and increase the power of sin or the power of righteousness, a change would certainly be made. Many would turn away from tradition and custom, and accept the divine principles of life.

POWER OF EXAMPLE

The physician who ministers in the homes of the people, watching at the bedside of the sick, relieving their distress, bringing them back from the borders of the grave, speaking hope to the dying, wins a place in their confidence and affection, such as is granted to few others. Not even to the minister of the gospel are committed possibilities so great or an influence so far-reaching.

The physician's example, no less than his teaching, should be a positive power on the right side. The cause of reform calls for men and women whose life practice is an illustration of self-control. It is our practice of the principles we inculcate that gives them weight. The world needs a practical demonstration of what the grace of God can do in restoring to human beings their lost kingship, giving them mastery of themselves. There is nothing that the world needs so much as a knowledge of the gospel's saving power revealed in Christlike lives. The physician is continually brought into contact with those who need the strength and encouragement of a right example. Many are weak in moral power. They lack self-control and are easily overcome by temptation. The physician can help these souls only as he reveals in his own life a strength of principle that enables him to triumph over every injurious habit and defiling lust. In his life must be seen the working of a power that is divine. If he fails here, however forcible or persuasive his words may be, his influence will tell for evil.

Many seek medical advice and treatment who have become moral wrecks through their own wrong habits. They are bruised and weak and wounded, feeling their folly and their inability to overcome. Such ones should have nothing in their surroundings to encourage a continuance of the thoughts and feelings that have made them what they are. They need to breathe an atmosphere of purity, of high and noble thought. How terrible the responsibility when those who should give them a right example are themselves enthralled by hurtful habits, their influence affording to temptation an added strength!

THE PHYSICIAN AND THE TEMPERANCE WORK

Many come under the physician's care who are ruining soul and body by the use of tobacco or intoxicating drink. The physician who is true to his responsibility must point out to these patients the cause of their suffering. But if he himself is a user of tobacco or intoxicants, what weight will be given to his words? With the consciousness of his own indulgence before him, will he not hesitate to point out the plague spot in the life of his patient? While using these things himself, how can he convince the youth of their injurious effects?

How can a physician stand in the community as an example of purity and self-control, how can he be an effectual worker in the temperance cause, while he himself is indulging a vile habit? How can he minister acceptably at the bedside of the sick and the dying, when his very breath is offensive, laden with the odor of liquor or tobacco?

While disordering his nerves and clouding his brain by the use of narcotic poisons, how can one be true to the trust reposed in him as a skillful physician? How impossible for him to discern quickly or to execute with precision!

If he does not observe the laws that govern his own being, if he chooses selfish gratification above soundness of mind and body, does he not thereby declare himself unfit to be entrusted with the responsibility of human lives?

However skilled and faithful a physician may be, there is in his experience much of apparent discouragement and defeat. Often his work fails of accomplishing that which he longs to see accomplished. Though health is restored to his patients, it may be no real benefit to them or to the world. Many recover health, only to repeat the indulgences that invited disease. With the same eagerness as before, they plunge again into the round of self-indulgence and folly.

The physician's work for them seems like effort thrown away.

Christ had the same experience, yet He did not cease His efforts for one suffering soul. Of the ten lepers who were cleansed, only one appreciated the gift, and he was a stranger and a Samaritan. For the sake of that one, Christ healed the ten. If the physician meets with no better success than the Saviour had, let him learn a lesson from the Chief Physician.

Of Christ it is written, "He shall not fail nor be discouraged." "He shall see of the travail of His soul, and shall be satisfied." Isaiah 42:4; 53:11.

If but one soul would have accepted the gospel of His grace, Christ would, to save that one, have chosen His life of toil and humiliation and His death of shame. If through our efforts one human being shall be uplifted and ennobled, fitted to shine in the courts of the Lord, have we not cause for rejoicing?

The duties of the physician are arduous and trying. In order to perform them most successfully he needs to have a strong constitution and vigorous health. A man that is feeble or diseased cannot endure the wearing labor incident to the physician's calling. One who lacks perfect self-control cannot become qualified to deal with all classes of disease.

Often deprived of sleep, neglecting even to take food, cut off in great degree from social enjoyment and religious privileges, the physician's life seems to lie under a continual shadow. The affliction he beholds, the dependent mortals longing for help, his contact with the depraved, make the heart sick, and well-nigh destroy confidence in humanity.

In the battle with disease and death every energy is taxed to the limit of endurance. The reaction from this terrible strain tests the character to the utmost. Then it is that temptation has greatest power. More than men in any other calling, is the physician in need of self-control, purity of spirit, and that faith which takes hold on heaven. For the sake of others and for his own sake, he cannot afford to disregard physical law. Recklessness in physical habits tends to recklessness in morals.

The physician's only safety is, under all circumstances, to act from principle, strengthened and ennobled by a firmness of purpose found only in God. He is to stand in the moral excellence of His character. Day by day, hour by hour, moment by moment, he is to live as in the sight of the unseen world. As did Moses, he must endure "as seeing Him who is invisible."

Righteousness has its root in godliness. No man can steadily maintain before his fellow men a pure, forceful life unless his life is hid with Christ in God. The greater the activity among men, the closer must be the communion of the heart with heaven.

The more urgent his duties and the greater his responsibilities, the greater the physician's need of divine power. Time must be redeemed from things temporal, for meditation upon things eternal. He must resist an encroaching world, which would so press upon him as to separate him from the Source of strength. Above all other men should he, by prayer and the study of the Scriptures, place himself under the protecting shield of God. He is to live in hourly contact and conscious communion with the principles of truth, righteousness, and mercy that reveal God's attributes within the soul.

Just to the degree in which the word of God is received and obeyed will it impress with its potency and touch with its life every spring of action, every phase of character. It will purify every thought, regulate every desire. Those who make God's word their trust will quit themselves like men and be strong. They will rise above all baser things into an atmosphere free from defilement.

When man is in fellowship with God, that unswerving purpose which preserved Joseph and Daniel amidst the corruption of heathen courts will make his a life of unsullied purity. His robes of character will be spotless. In his life the light of Christ will be undimmed. The bright and morning Star will appear shining steadfastly above him in changeless glory.

Such a life will be an element of strength in the community. It will be a barrier against evil, a safeguard to the tempted, a guiding light to those who, amidst difficulties and discouragements, are seeking the right way.

TEACHING AND HEALING

When Christ sent out the twelve disciples on their first missionary tour, He bade them, "As ye go, preach, saying, The kingdom of heaven is at hand. Heal the sick, cleanse the lepers, raise the dead, cast out devils: freely ye have received, freely give." Matthew 10:7, 8.

To the Seventy sent forth later He said: "Into whatsoever city ye enter, heal the sick that are therein, and say unto them, The kingdom of God is come nigh unto you." Luke 10:8, 9. The presence and power of Christ was with them, "and the Seventy returned again with joy, saying, Lord, even the devils are subject unto us through Thy name." Verse 17.

After Christ's ascension the same work was continued. The scenes of His own ministry were repeated. "Out of the cities round about" there came a multitude "unto Jerusalem, bringing sick folks, and them which were vexed with unclean spirits: and they were healed every one." Acts 5:16.

And the disciples "went forth, and preached everywhere, the Lord working with them." "Philip went down to the city of Samaria, and preached Christ unto them. And the people with one accord gave heed unto those things which Philip spake. . . . For unclean spirits . . . came out of many that were possessed with them: and many taken with palsies, and that were lame, were healed. And there was great joy in that city." Mark 16:20; Acts 8:5-8.

WORK OF THE DISCIPLES

Luke, the writer of the Gospel that bears his name, was a medical missionary. In the Scriptures he is called "the beloved physician." Colossians 4:14. The apostle Paul heard of his skill as a physician, and sought him out as one to whom the Lord had entrusted a special work. He secured his co-operation, and for some time Luke accompanied him in his travels from place to place. After a time, Paul left Luke at Philippi, in Macedonia. Here he continued to labor for several years, both as a physician and as a teacher of the gospel. In his work as a physician he ministered to the sick, and then prayed for the healing power of God to rest upon the afflicted ones. Thus the way was opened for the gospel message. Luke's success as a physician gained for him many opportunities for preaching Christ among the heathen. It is the divine plan that we shall work as the disciples worked. Physical healing is bound up with the gospel commission. In the work of the gospel, teaching and healing are never to be separated.

The work of the disciples was to spread a knowledge of the gospel. To them was committed the work of proclaiming to all the world the good news that Christ brought to men. That work they accomplished for the people of their time. To every nation under heaven the gospel was carried in a single generation.

The giving of the gospel to the world is the work that God has committed to those who bear His name. For earth's sin and misery the gospel is the only antidote. To make known to all mankind the message of the grace of God is the first work of those who know its healing power.

When Christ sent forth the disciples with the gospel message, faith in God and His word had well-nigh departed from the world. Among the Jewish people, who professed to have a knowledge of Jehovah, His word had been set aside for tradition and human speculation. Selfish ambition, love of ostentation, greed of gain, absorbed men's thoughts. As reverence for God departed, so also departed compassion toward men. Selfishness was the ruling principle, and Satan worked his will in the misery and degradation of mankind.

Satanic agencies took possession of men. The bodies of human beings, made for the dwelling place of God, became the habitation of demons. The senses, the nerves, the organs of men were worked by supernatural agencies in the indulgence of the vilest lust. The very stamp of demons was impressed upon the countenances of men. Human faces reflected the expression of the legions of evil with which men were possessed.

What is the condition in the world today? Is not faith in the Bible as effectually destroyed by the higher criticism and speculation of today as it was by tradition and rabbinism in the days of Christ? Have not greed and ambition and love of pleasure as strong a hold on men's hearts now as they had then? In the professedly Christian world, even in the professed churches of Christ, how few are governed by

Christian principles. In business, social, domestic, even religious circles, how few make the teachings of Christ the rule of daily living. Is it not true that "justice standeth afar off... equity cannot enter... And he that departeth from evil maketh himself a prey"? Isaiah 59:14, 15.

We are living in the midst of an "epidemic of crime," at which thoughtful, God-fearing men everywhere stand aghast. The corruption that prevails, it is beyond the power of the human pen to describe. Every day brings fresh revelations of political strife, bribery, and fraud. Every day brings its heart-sickening record of violence and lawlessness, of indifference to human suffering, of brutal, fiendish destruction of human life. Every day testifies to the increase of insanity, murder, and suicide. Who can doubt that satanic agencies are at work among men with increasing activity to distract and corrupt the mind, and defile and destroy the body?

And while the world is filled with these evils, the gospel is too often presented in so indifferent a manner as to make but little impression upon the consciences or the lives of men. Everywhere there are hearts crying out for something which they have not. They long for a power that will give them mastery over sin, a power that will deliver them from the bondage of evil, a power that will give health and life and peace. Many who once knew the power of God's word have dwelt where there is no recognition of God, and they long for the divine presence.

The world needs today what it needed nineteen hundred years ago–a revelation of Christ. A great work of reform is demanded, and it is only through the grace of Christ that the work of restoration, physical, mental, and spiritual, can be accomplished. Christ's method alone will give true success in reaching the people. The Saviour mingled with men as one who desired their good. He showed His sympathy for them, ministered to their needs, and won their confidence. Then He bade them, "Follow Me."

There is need of coming close to the people by personal effort. If less time were given to sermonizing, and more time were spent in personal ministry, greater results would be seen. The poor are to be relieved, the sick cared for, the sorrowing and the bereaved comforted, the ignorant instructed, the inexperienced counseled. We are to weep with those that weep, and rejoice with those that rejoice.

Accompanied by the power of persuasion, the power of prayer, the power of the love of God, this work will not, cannot, be without fruit.

We should ever remember that the object of the medical missionary work is to point sin-sick men and women to the Man of Calvary, who taketh away the sin of the world. By beholding Him, they will be changed into His likeness. We are to encourage the sick and suffering to look to Jesus and live. Let the workers keep Christ, the Great Physician, constantly before those to whom disease of body and soul has brought discouragement. Point them to the One who can heal both physical and spiritual disease. Tell them of the One who is touched with the feeling of their infirmities. Encourage them to place themselves in the care of Him who gave His life to make it possible for them to have life eternal. Talk of His love; tell of His power to save.

This is the high duty and precious privilege of the medical missionary. And personal ministry often prepares the way for this. God often reaches hearts through our efforts to relieve physical suffering.

Medical missionary work is the pioneer work of the gospel. In the ministry of the word and in the medical missionary work the gospel is to be preached and practiced.

In almost every community there are large numbers who do not listen to the preaching of God's word or attend any religious service. If they are reached by the gospel, it must be carried to their homes. Often the relief of their physical needs is the only avenue by which they can be approached. Missionary nurses who care for the sick and relieve the distress of the poor will find many opportunities to pray with them, to read to them from God's word, and to speak of the Saviour. They can pray with and for the helpless ones who have not strength of will to control the appetites that passion has degraded. They can bring a ray of hope into the lives of the defeated and disheartened. Their unselfish love, manifested in acts of disinterested kindness, will make it easier for these suffering ones to believe in the love of Christ.

Many have no faith in God and have lost confidence in man. But they appreciate acts of sympathy and helpfulness. As they see one with no inducement of earthly praise or compensation come into their homes, ministering to the sick, feeding the hungry, clothing the naked, comforting the sad, and tenderly pointing all to Him of whose love and pity the human worker is but the messenger–as they see this, their hearts are touched. Gratitude springs up. Faith is kindled. They see that God cares for them, and they are prepared to listen as His word is opened.

Whether in foreign missions or in the home field, all missionaries, both men and women, will gain much more ready access to the people, and will find their usefulness greatly increased, if they are able to minister to the sick. Women who go as missionaries to heathen lands may thus find opportunity for giving the gospel to the women of these lands, when every other door of access is closed. All gospel workers should know how to give the simple treatments that do so much to relieve pain and remove disease.

TEACHING HEALTH PRINCIPLES

Gospel workers should be able also to give instruction in the principles of healthful living. There is sickness everywhere, and most of it might be prevented by attention to the laws of health. The people need to see the bearing of health principles upon their well-being, both for this life and for the life to come. They need to be awakened to their responsibility for the human habitation fitted up by their Creator as His dwelling place, and over which He desires them to be faithful stewards. They need to be impressed with the truth conveyed in the words of Holy Writ: "Ye are the temple of the living God; as God hath said, I will dwell in them, and walk in them; and I will be their God, and they shall be My people." 2 Corinthians 6:16. Thousands need and would gladly receive instruction concerning the simple methods of treating the sick–methods that are taking the place of the use of poisonous drugs. There is great need of instruction in regard to dietetic reform. Wrong habits of eating and the use of unhealthful food are in no small degree responsible for the intemperance and crime and wretchedness that curse the world.

In teaching health principles, keep before the mind the great object of reform–that its purpose is to secure the highest development of body and mind and soul. Show that the laws of nature, being the laws of God, are designed for our good; that obedience to them promotes happiness in this life, and aids in the preparation for the life to come.

Lead the people to study the manifestation of God's love and wisdom in the works of nature. Lead them to study that marvelous organism, the human system, and the laws by which it is governed. Those who perceive the evidences of God's love, who understand something of the wisdom and beneficence of His laws, and the results of obedience, will come to regard their duties and obligations from an altogether different point of view. Instead of looking upon an observance of the laws of health as a matter of sacrifice or self-denial, they will regard it, as it really is, as an inestimable blessing.

Every gospel worker should feel that the giving of instruction in the principles of healthful living is a part of his appointed work. Of this work there is great need, and the world is open for it.

Everywhere there is a tendency to substitute the work of organizations for individual effort. Human wisdom tends to consolidation, to centralization, to the building up of great churches and institutions. Multitudes leave to institutions and organizations the work of benevolence; they excuse themselves from contact with the world, and their hearts grow cold. They become self-absorbed and unimpressible. Love for God and man dies out of the soul.

Christ commits to His followers an individual work–a work that cannot be done by proxy. Ministry to the sick and the poor, the giving of the gospel to the lost, is not to be left to committees or organized charities. Individual responsibility, individual effort, personal sacrifice, is the requirement of the gospel.

"Go out into the highways and hedges, and compel them to come in," is Christ's command, "that My house may be filled." He brings men into touch with those whom they seek to benefit. "Bring the poor that are cast out to thy house," He says. "When thou seest the naked, that thou cover him." "They shall lay hands on the sick, and they shall recover." Luke 14: 23; Isaiah 58:7; Mark 16:18. Through direct contact, through personal ministry, the blessings of the gospel are to be communicated.

In giving light to His people anciently, God did not work exclusively through any one class. Daniel was a prince of Judah. Isaiah also was of the royal line. David was a shepherd boy, Amos a herdsman, Zechariah a captive from Babylon, Elisha a tiller of the soil.

The Lord raised up as His representatives prophets and princes, the noble and the lowly, and taught them the truths to be given to the world.

To everyone who becomes a partaker of His grace the Lord appoints a work for others. Individually we are to stand in our lot and place, saying, "Here am I; send me." Isaiah 6:8. Upon the minister of the word, the missionary nurse, the Christian physician, the individual Christian, whether he be merchant or farmer, professional man or mechanic–the responsibility rests upon all. It is our work to reveal to men the gospel of their salvation. Every enterprise in which we engage should be a means to this end.

Those who take up their appointed work will not only be a blessing to others, but they will themselves be blessed. The consciousness of duty well done will have a reflex influence upon their own souls. The despondent will forget their despondency, the weak will become strong, the ignorant intelligent, and all will find an unfailing helper in Him who has called them.

The church of Christ is organized for service. Its watchword is ministry. Its members are soldiers, to be trained for conflict under the Captain of their salvation. Christian ministers, physicians, teachers, have a broader work than many have recognized. They are not only to minister to the people, but to teach them to minister. They should not only give instruction in right principles, but educate their hearers to impart these principles. Truth that is not lived, that is not imparted, loses its life-giving power, its healing virtue. Its blessing can be retained only as it is shared.

The monotony of our service for God needs to be broken up. Every church member should be engaged in some line of service for the Master. Some cannot do so much as others, but everyone should do his utmost to roll back the tide of disease and distress that is sweeping over our world. Many would be willing to work if they were taught how to begin.

They need to be instructed and encouraged. Every church should be a training school for Christian workers. Its members should be taught how to give Bible readings, how to conduct and teach Sabbath-school classes, how best to help the poor and to care for the sick, how to work for the unconverted. There should be schools of health, cooking schools, and classes in various lines of Christian help work. There should not only be teaching, but actual work under experienced instructors. Let the teachers lead the way in working among the people, and others, uniting with them, will learn from their example. One example is worth more than many precepts.

Let all cultivate their physical and mental powers to the utmost of their ability, that they may work for God where His providence shall call them. The same grace that came from Christ to Paul and Apollos, that distinguished them for spiritual excellencies, will today be imparted to devoted Christian missionaries. God desires His children to have intelligence and knowledge, that with unmistakable clearness and power His glory may be revealed in our world.

Educated workers who are consecrated to God can do service in a greater variety of ways and can accomplish more extensive work than can those who are uneducated. Their discipline of mind places them on vantage ground. But those who have neither great talents nor extensive education may minister acceptably to others. God will use men who are willing to be used. It is not the most brilliant or the most talented persons whose work produces the greatest and most lasting results. Men and women are needed who have heard a message from heaven. The most effective workers are those who respond to the invitation, "Take My yoke upon you, and learn of Me." Matthew 11:29.

It is heart missionaries that are needed. He whose heart God touches is filled with a great longing for those who have never known His love. Their condition impresses him with a sense of personal woe. Taking his life in his hand, he goes forth, a heaven-sent, heaven-inspired messenger, to do a work in which angels can co-operate.

If those to whom God has entrusted great talents of intellect put these gifts to a selfish use, they will be left, after a period of trial, to follow their own way. God will take men who do not appear to be so richly endowed, who have not large self-confidence, and He will make the weak strong, because they trust in Him to do for them that which they cannot do for themselves. God will accept the wholehearted service, and will Himself make up the deficiencies.

The Lord has often chosen for His colaborers men who have had opportunity to obtain but a limited school education. These men have applied their powers most diligently, and the Lord has rewarded their fidelity to His work, their industry, their thirst for knowledge. He has witnessed their tears and heard their prayers. As His blessing came to the captives in the courts of Babylon, so does He give wisdom and knowledge to His workers today.

Men deficient in school education, lowly in social position, have, through the grace of Christ, sometimes been wonderfully successful in winning souls for Him. The secret of their success was their confidence in God. They learned daily of Him who is wonderful in counsel and mighty in power.

Such workers are to be encouraged. The Lord brings them into connection with those of more marked ability, to fill up the gaps that others leave. Their quickness to see what is to be done, their readiness to help those in need, their kind words and deeds, open doors of usefulness that otherwise would remain closed. They come close to those in trouble, and the persuasive influence of their words has power to draw many trembling souls to God. Their work shows what thousands of others might do, if they only would.

A BROADER LIFE

Nothing will so arouse a self-sacrificing zeal and broaden and strengthen the character as to engage in work for others. Many professed Christians, in seeking church relationship, think only of themselves. They wish to enjoy church fellowship and pastoral care. They become members of large and prosperous churches, and are content to do little for others. In this way they are robbing themselves of the most precious blessings. Many would be greatly benefited by sacrificing their pleasant, ease-conducing associations. They need to go where their energies will be called out in Christian work and they can learn to bear responsibilities.

Trees that are crowded closely together do not grow healthfully and sturdily. The gardener transplants them that they may have room to develop. A similar work would benefit many of the members of large churches. They need to be placed where their energies will be called forth in active Christian effort. They are losing their spiritual life, becoming dwarfed and inefficient, for want of self-sacrificing labor for others. Transplanted to some missionary field, they would grow strong and vigorous.

But none need wait until called to some distant field before beginning to help others. Doors of service are open everywhere. All around us are those who need our help. The widow, the orphan, the sick and the dying, the heartsick, the discouraged, the ignorant, and the outcast are on every hand.

We should feel it our special duty to work for those living in our neighborhood. Study how you can best help those who take no interest in religious things. As you visit your friends and neighbors, show an interest in their spiritual as well as in their temporal welfare. Speak to them of Christ as a sin-pardoning Saviour. Invite your neighbors to your home, and read with them from the precious Bible and from books that explain its truths. Invite them to unite with you in song and prayer. In these little gatherings, Christ Himself will be present, as He has promised, and hearts will be touched by His grace.

Church members should educate themselves to do this work. This is just as essential as to save the benighted souls in foreign countries. While some feel the burden for souls afar off, let the many who are at home feel the burden of precious souls who are around them, and work just as diligently for their salvation.

Many regret that they are living a narrow life. They themselves can make their life broad and influential if they will. Those who love Jesus with heart and mind and soul, and their neighbor as themselves, have a wide field in which to use their ability and influence.

LITTLE OPPORTUNITIES

Let none pass by little opportunities, to look for larger work. You might do successfully the small work, but fail utterly in attempting the larger work, and fall into discouragement. It is by doing with your might what you find to do that you will develop aptitude for larger work. It is by slighting the daily opportunities, by neglecting the little things right at hand, that so many become fruitless and withered.

Do not depend upon human aid. Look beyond human beings to the One appointed by God to bear our griefs, to carry our sorrows, and to supply our necessities. Taking God at His word, make a beginning wherever you find work to do, and move forward with unfaltering faith. It is faith in Christ's presence that gives strength and steadfastness. Work with unselfish interest, with painstaking effort, with persevering energy.

In fields where the conditions are so objectionable and disheartening that many are unwilling to go to them, remarkable changes have been wrought by the efforts of self-sacrificing workers. Patiently and perseveringly they labored, not relying upon human power, but upon God, and His grace sustained them. The amount of good thus accomplished will never be known in this world, but blessed results will be seen in the great hereafter.

SELF-SUPPORTING MISSIONARIES

In many places self-supporting missionaries can work successfully. It was as a self-supporting missionary that the apostle Paul labored in spreading the knowledge of Christ throughout the world. While daily teaching the gospel in the great cities of Asia and Europe, he wrought at the trade of a craftsman to sustain himself and his companions. His parting words to the elders of Ephesus, showing his manner of labor, have precious lessons for every gospel worker:

"Ye know," he said, "after what manner I have been with you at all seasons:... and how I kept back nothing that was profitable unto you, but have showed you, and have taught you publicly, and from house to house... I have coveted no man's silver, or gold, or apparel. Yea, ye yourselves know, that these hands have ministered unto my necessities, and to them that were with me. I have showed you all things, how that so laboring ye ought to support the weak, and to remember the words of the Lord Jesus, how He said, It is more blessed to give than to receive." Acts 20:18-35.

Many today, if imbued with the same spirit of self-sacrifice, could do a good work in a similar way. Let two or more start out together in evangelistic work. Let them visit the people, praying, singing, teaching, explaining the Scriptures, and ministering to the sick. Some can sustain themselves as canvassers; others, like the apostle, can labor at some handicraft or in other lines of effort. As they move forward in their work, realizing their helplessness, but humbly depending upon God, they gain a blessed experience. The Lord Jesus goes before them, and among the wealthy and the poor they find favor and help.

Those who have been trained for medical missionary work in

foreign countries should be encouraged to go without delay where they expect to labor, and begin work among the people, learning the language as they work. Very soon they will be able to teach the simple truths of God's word.

Throughout the world, messengers of mercy are needed. There is a call for Christian families to go into communities that are in darkness and error, to go to foreign fields, to become acquainted with the needs of their fellow men, and to work for the cause of the Master. If such families would settle in the dark places of the earth, places where the people are enshrouded in spiritual gloom, and let the light of Christ's life shine out through them, what a noble work might be accomplished.

This work requires self-sacrifice. While many are waiting to have every obstacle removed, the work they might do is left undone, and multitudes are dying without hope and without God. Some for the sake of commercial advantage, or to acquire scientific knowledge, will venture into unsettled regions and cheerfully endure sacrifice and hardship; but how few for the sake of their fellow men are willing to move their families into regions that are in need of the gospel.

To reach the people, wherever they are, and whatever their position or condition, and to help them in every way possible –this is true ministry. By such effort you may win hearts and open a door of access to perishing souls.

In all your work remember that you are bound up with Christ, a part of the great plan of redemption. The love of Christ, in a healing, life-giving current, is to flow through your life. As you seek to draw others within the circle of His love, let the purity of your language, the unselfishness of your service, the joyfulness of your demeanor, bear witness to the power of His grace. Give to the world so pure and righteous a representation of Him, that men shall behold Him in His beauty.

It is of little use to try to reform others by attacking what we may regard as wrong habits. Such effort often results in more harm than good. In His talk with the Samaritan woman, instead of disparaging Jacob's well, Christ presented something better. "If thou knewest the gift of God," He said, "and who it is that saith to thee, Give Me to drink; thou wouldest have asked of Him, and He would have given thee living water." John 4:10. He turned the conversation to the treasure He had to bestow, offering the woman something better than she possessed, even living water, the joy and hope of the gospel.

This is an illustration of the way in which we are to work. We must offer men something better than that which they possess, even the peace of Christ, which passeth all understanding. We must tell them of God's holy law, the transcript of His character, and an expression of that which He wishes them to become. Show them how infinitely superior to the fleeting joys and pleasures of the world is the imperishable glory of heaven. Tell them of the freedom and rest to be found in the Saviour. "Whosoever drinketh of the water that I shall give him shall never thirst," He daclared. Verse 14.

Lift up Jesus, crying, "Behold, the Lamb of God, that taketh away the sin of the world!" John 1:29, A.R.V. He alone can satisfy the craving of the heart and give peace to the soul.

Of all people in the world, reformers should be the most unselfish, the most kind, the most courteous. In their lives should be seen the true goodness of unselfish deeds. The worker who manifests a lack of courtesy, who shows impatience at the ignorance or waywardness of others, who speaks hastily or acts thoughtlessly, may close the door to hearts so that he can never reach them.

As the dew and the still showers fall upon the withering plants, so let words fall gently when seeking to win men from error. God's plan is first to reach the heart. We are to speak the truth in love, trusting in Him to give it power for the reforming of the life. The Holy Spirit will apply to the soul the word that is spoken in love.

Naturally we are self-centered and opinionated. But when we learn the lessons that Christ desires to teach us, we become partakers of His nature; henceforth we live His life. The wonderful example of Christ, the matchless tenderness with which He entered into the feelings of others, weeping with those who wept, rejoicing with those who rejoiced, must have a deep influence upon the character of all who follow Him in sincerity. By kindly words and acts they will try to make the path easy for weary feet.

"The Lord Eternal hath given me a tongue for teaching."

"That I should know how to speak a word in season to him that is weary." Isaiah 50:4, Leeser's Translation.

All around us are afflicted souls. Here and there, everywhere, we may find them. Let us search out these suffering ones and speak a word in season to comfort their hearts. Let us ever be channels through which shall flow the refreshing waters of compassion.

In all our associations it should be remembered that in the experience of others there are chapters sealed from mortal sight. On the pages of memory are sad histories that are sacredly guarded from curious eyes. There stand registered long, hard battles with trying circumstances, perhaps troubles in the home life, that day by day weaken courage, confidence, and faith. Those who are fighting the battle of life at great odds may be strengthened and encouraged by little attentions that cost only a loving effort. To such the strong, helpful grasp of the hand by a true friend is worth more than gold or silver. Words of kindness are as welcome as the smile of angels.

There are multitudes struggling with poverty, compelled to labor hard for small wages, and able to secure but the barest necessities of life. Toil and deprivation, with no hope of better things, make their burden very heavy. When pain and sickness are added, the burden is almost insupportable. Careworn and oppressed, they know not where to turn for relief. Sympathize with them in their trials, their heartaches, and disappointments. This will open the way for you to help them. Speak to them of God's promises, pray with and for them, inspire them with hope.

Words of cheer and encouragement spoken when the soul is sick and the pulse of courage is low–these are regarded by the Saviour as if spoken to Himself. As hearts are cheered, the heavenly angels look on in pleased recognition.

From age to age the Lord has been seeking to awaken in the souls of men a sense of their divine brotherhood. Be co-workers with Him. While distrust and alienation are pervading the world, Christ's disciples are to reveal the spirit that reigns in heaven.

Speak as He would speak, act as He would act. Constantly reveal the sweetness of His character. Reveal that wealth of love which underlies all His teachings and all His dealings with men. The humblest workers, in co-operation with Christ, may touch chords whose vibrations shall ring to the ends of the earth and make melody throughout eternal ages.

Heavenly intelligences are waiting to co-operate with human instrumentalities, that they may reveal to the world what human beings may become, and what, through union with the Divine, may be accomplished for the saving of souls that are ready to perish. There is no limit to the usefulness of one who, putting self aside, makes room for the working of the Holy Spirit upon his heart and lives a life wholly consecrated to God. All who consecrate body, soul, and spirit to His service will be constantly receiving a new endowment of physical, mental, and spiritual power. The inexhaustible supplies of heaven are at their command. Christ gives them the breath of His own Spirit, the life of His own life. The Holy Spirit puts forth its highest energies to work in mind and heart. Through the grace given us we may achieve victories that because of our own erroneous and preconceived opinions, our defects of character, our smallness of faith, have seemed impossible.

To everyone who offers himself to the Lord for service, withholding nothing, is given power for the attainment of measureless results. For these God will do great things. He will work upon the minds of men so that, even in this world, there shall be seen in their lives a fulfillment of the promise of the future state. See Isaiah 35:1-10

GENERAL HYGIENE

The knowledge that man is to be a temple for God, a habitation for the revealing of His glory, should be the highest incentive to the care and development of our physical powers. Fearfully and wonderfully has the Creator wrought in the human frame, and He bids us make it our study, understand its needs, and act our part in preserving it from harm and defilement.

THE CIRCULATION OF THE BLOOD

In order to have good health, we must have good blood; for the blood is the current of life. It repairs waste and nourishes the body. When supplied with the proper food elements and when cleansed and vitalized by contact with pure air, it carries life and vigor to every part of the system. The more perfect the circulation, the better will this work be accomplished.

At every pulsation of the heart the blood should make its way quickly and easily to all parts of the body. Its circulation should not be hindered by tight clothing or bands, or by insufficient clothing of the extremities. Whatever hinders the circulation forces the blood back to the vital organs, producing congestion. Headache, cough, palpitation of the heart, or indigestion is often the result.

RESPIRATION

In order to have good blood, we must breathe well. Full, deep inspirations of pure air, which fill the lungs with oxygen, purify the blood. They impart to it a bright color and send it, a life-giving current, to every part of the body. A good respiration soothes the nerves; it stimulates the appetite and renders digestion more perfect; and it induces sound, refreshing sleep.

The lungs should be allowed the greatest freedom possible. Their capacity is developed by free action; it diminishes if they are cramped and compressed. Hence the ill effects of the practice so common, especially in sedentary pursuits, of stooping at one's work. In this position it is impossible to breathe deeply. Superficial breathing soon becomes a habit, and the lungs lose their power to expand. A similar effect is produced by tight lacing. Sufficient room is not given to the lower part of the chest; the abdominal muscles, which were designed to aid in breathing, do not have full play, and the lungs are restricted in their action.

Thus an insufficient supply of oxygen is received. The blood moves sluggishly. The waste, poisonous matter, which should be thrown off in the exhalations from the lungs, is retained, and the blood becomes impure. Not only the lungs, but the stomach, liver, and brain are affected. The skin becomes sallow, digestion is retarded; the heart is depressed; the brain is clouded; the thoughts are confused; gloom settles upon the spirits; the whole system becomes depressed and inactive, and peculiarly susceptible to disease.

The lungs are constantly throwing off impurities, and they need to be constantly supplied with fresh air. Impure air does not afford the necessary supply of oxygen, and the blood passes to the brain and other organs without being vitalized. Hence the necessity of thorough ventilation. To live in close, ill-ventilated rooms, where the air is dead and vitiated, weakens the entire system. It becomes peculiarly sensitive to the influence of cold, and a slight exposure induces disease. It is close confinement indoors that makes many women pale and feeble. They breathe the same air over and over until it becomes laden with poisonous matter thrown off through the lungs and pores, and impurities are thus conveyed back to the blood.

VENTILATION AND SUNLIGHT

In the construction of buildings, whether for public purposes or as dwellings, care should be taken to provide for good ventilation and plenty of sunlight. Churches and schoolrooms are often faulty in this respect. Neglect of proper ventilation is responsible for much of the drowsiness and dullness that destroy the effect of many a sermon and make the teacher's work toilsome and ineffective.

So far as possible, all buildings intended for human habitation should be placed on high, well-drained ground. This will ensure a dry site and prevent the danger of disease from dampness and miasma. This matter is often too lightly regarded. Continuous ill-health, serious diseases, and many deaths result from the dampness and malaria of low-lying, ill-drained situations.

In the building of houses it is especially important to secure thorough ventilation and plenty of sunlight. Let there be a current of air and an abundance of light in every room in the house. Sleeping rooms should be so arranged as to have a free circulation of air day and night. No room is fit to be occupied as a sleeping room unless it can be thrown open daily to the air and sunshine. In most countries bedrooms need to be supplied with conveniences for heating, that they may be thoroughly warmed and dried in cold or wet weather.

The guestchamber should have equal care with the rooms intended for constant use. Like the other bedrooms, it should have air and sunshine, and should be provided with some means of heating, to dry out the dampness that always accumulates in a room not in constant use. Whoever sleeps in a sunless room, or occupies a bed that has not been thoroughly dried and aired, does so at the risk of health, and often of life.

In building, many make careful provision for their plants and flowers. The greenhouse or window devoted to their use is warm and sunny; for without warmth, air, and sunshine, plants would not live and flourish. If these conditions are necessary to the life of plants, how much more necessary are they for our own health and that of our families and guests!

If we would have our homes the abiding place of health and happiness we must place them above the miasma and fog of the lowlands, and give free entrance to heaven's life-giving agencies. Dispense with heavy curtains, open the windows and the blinds, allow no vines, however beautiful, to shade the windows, and permit no trees to stand so near the house as to shut out the sunshine. The sunlight may fade the drapery and the carpets, and tarnish the picture frames; but it will bring a healthy glow to the cheeks of the children.

Those who have the aged to provide for should remember that these especially need warm, comfortable rooms. Vigor declines as years advance, leaving less vitality with which to resist unhealthful influences; hence the greater necessity for the aged to have plenty of sunlight, and fresh, pure air.

Scrupulous cleanliness is essential to both physical and mental health. Impurities are constantly thrown off from the body through the skin. Its millions of pores are quickly clogged unless kept clean by frequent bathing, and the impurities which should pass off through the skin become an additional burden to the other eliminating organs.

Most persons would receive benefit from a cool or tepid bath every day, morning or evening. Instead of increasing the liability to take cold, a bath, properly taken, fortifies against cold, because it improves the circulation; the blood is brought to the surface, and a more easy and regular flow is obtained. The mind and the body are alike invigorated. The muscles become more flexible, the intellect is made brighter. The bath is a soother of the nerves. Bathing helps the bowels, the stomach, and the liver, giving health and energy to each, and it promotes digestion.

It is important also that the clothing be kept clean. The garments worn absorb the waste matter that passes off through the pores; if they are not frequently changed and washed, the impurities will be reabsorbed.

Every form of uncleanliness tends to disease. Death-producing germs abound in dark, neglected corners, in decaying refuse, in dampness and mold and must. No waste vegetables or heaps of fallen leaves should be allowed to remain near the house to decay and poison the air. Nothing unclean or decaying should be tolerated within the home. In towns or cities regarded perfectly healthful, many an epidemic of fever has been traced to decaying matter about the dwelling of some careless householder.

Perfect cleanliness, plenty of sunlight, careful attention to sanitation in every detail of the home life, are essential to freedom from disease and to the cheerfulness and vigor of the inmates of the home.

HYGIENE AMONG THE ANCIENT AFRICAN HEBREWS

In the teaching that God gave to [the African Hebrews], the preservation of health received careful attention. The people who had come from slavery with the uncleanly and unhealthful habits which it engenders, were subjected to the strictest training in the wilderness before entering Canaan. Health principles were taught and sanitary laws enforced.

PREVENTION OF DISEASE

Not only in their religious service, but in all the affairs of daily life was observed the distinction between clean and unclean. All who came in contact with contagious or contaminating diseases were isolated from the encampment, and they were not permitted to return without thorough cleansing of both the person and the clothing. In the case of one afflicted with a contaminating disease, the direction was given:

"Every bed, whereon he lieth, . . . is unclean: and everything, whereon he sitteth, shall be unclean. And whosoever toucheth his bed shall wash his clothes, and bathe himself in water, and be unclean until the even. And he that sitteth on anything whereon he sat . . . shall wash his clothes, and bathe himself in water, and be unclean until the even. And he that toucheth the flesh of him . . . shall wash his clothes, and bathe himself in water, and be unclean until the even. . . . And whosoever toucheth anything that was under him shall be unclean until the even: and he that beareth any of those things shall wash his clothes, and bathe himself in water, and be unclean until the even. And whomsoever he toucheth . . . and hath not rinsed his hands in water, he shall wash his clothes, and bathe himself in water, and be unclean until the even. And the vessel of earth, that he toucheth, . . . shall be broken: and every vessel of wood shall be rinsed in water." Leviticus 15:4-12. The law concerning leprosy is also an illustration of the thoroughness with which these regulations were to be enforced:

"All the days wherein the plague shall be in him [the leper] he shall be defiled; he is unclean: he shall dwell alone; without the camp shall his habitation be. The garment also that the plague of leprosy is in, whether it be a woolen garment, or a linen garment; whether it be in the warp, or woof; of linen, or of woolen; whether in a skin, or in anything made of skin; . . . the priest shall look upon the plague: . . . if the plague be spread in the garment, either in the warp, or in the woof, or in a skin, or in any work that is made of skin; the plague is a fretting leprosy; it is unclean. He shall therefore burn that garment, whether warp or woof, in woolen or in linen, or anything of skin, wherein the plague is: for it is a fretting leprosy; it shall be burnt in the fire." Leviticus 13:46-52.

So, too, if a house gave evidence of conditions that rendered it unsafe for habitation, it was destroyed. The priest was to "break down the house, the stones of it, and the timber thereof, and all the mortar of the house; and he shall carry them forth out of the city into an unclean place. Moreover he that goeth into the house all the while that it is shut up shall be unclean until the even. And he that lieth in the house shall wash his clothes; and he that eateth in the house shall wash his clothes." Leviticus 14:45-47.

CLEANLINESS

The necessity of personal cleanliness was taught in the most impressive manner. Before gathering at Mount Sinai to listen to the proclamation of the law by the voice of God, the people were required to wash both their persons and their clothing. This direction was enforced on pain of death. No impurity was to be tolerated in the presence of God.

During the sojourn in the wilderness the [African Hebrews] were almost continually in the open air, where impurities would have a less harmful effect than upon the dwellers in close houses. But the strictest regard to cleanliness was required both within and without their tents. No refuse was allowed to remain within or about the encampment. The Lord said: "The Lord thy God walketh in the midst of thy camp, to deliver thee, and to give up thine enemies before thee; therefore shall thy camp be holy." Deuteronomy 23:14.

DIET

The distinction between clean and unclean was made in all matters of diet: "I am the Lord thy God, which have separated you from other people. Ye shall therefore put difference between clean beasts and unclean, and between unclean fowls and clean: and ye shall not make your souls abominable by beast, or by fowl, or by any manner of living thing, . . . which I have separated from you as unclean." Leviticus 20:24, 25.

Many articles of food eaten freely by the heathen about them were forbidden to the Israelites. It was no arbitrary distinction that was made. The things prohibited were unwholesome. And the fact that they were pronounced unclean taught the lesson that the use of injurious foods is defiling. That which corrupts the body tends to corrupt the soul. It unfits the user for communion with God, unfits him for high and holy service.

In the Promised Land the discipline begun in the wilderness was continued under circumstances favorable to the formation of right habits. The people were not crowded together in cities, but each family had its own landed possession, ensuring to all the health-giving blessings of a natural, unperverted life.

Concerning the cruel, licentious practices of the Canaanites, who were dispossessed by [the African Hebrews], the Lord said: "Ye shall not walk in the manners of the nation, which I cast out before you: for they committed all these things, and therefore I abhorred them." Verse 23. "Neither shalt thou bring an abomination into thine house, lest thou be a cursed thing like it." Deuteronomy 7:26.

In all the affairs of their daily life, the Israelites were taught the lesson set forth by the Holy Spirit: "Know ye not that ye are the temple of God, and that the Spirit of God dwelleth in you? If any man defile the temple of God, him shall God destroy; for the temple of God is holy, which temple ye are." 1 Corinthians 3:16, 17.

REJOICING

"A merry [rejoicing] heart doeth good like a medicine." Proverbs 17:22. Gratitude, rejoicing, benevolence, trust in God's love and care–these are health's greatest safeguard. To the [African Hebrews] they were to be the very keynote of life.

The journey made three times a year to the annual feasts at Jerusalem, the week's sojourn in booths during the Feast of Tabernacles, were opportunities for outdoor recreation and social life. These feasts were occasions of rejoicing, made sweeter and more tender by the hospitable welcome given to the stranger, the Levite, and the poor.

"Rejoice in every good thing which the Lord thy God hath given unto thee, and unto thine house, thou, and the Levite, and the stranger that is among you." Deuteronomy 26:11.

So, in later years, when the law of God was read in Jerusalem to the captives returned from Babylon, and the people wept because of their transgressions, the gracious words were spoken:

"Mourn not. . . . Go your way, eat the fat, and drink the sweet, and send portions unto them for whom nothing is prepared: for this day is holy unto our Lord: neither be ye sorry; for the joy of the Lord is your strength." Nehemiah 8:9, 10.

And it was published and proclaimed "in all their cities, and in Jerusalem, saying, Go forth unto the mount, and fetch olive branches, and pine branches, and myrtle branches, and palm branches, and branches of thick trees, to make booths, as it is written. So the people went forth, and brought them, and made themselves booths, everyone upon the roof of his house, and in their courts, and in the courts of the house of God, and in the street of the water gate, and in the street of the gate of Ephraim. And all the congregation of them that were come again out of the captivity made booths, and sat under the booths. ... And there was very great gladness." Verses 15-17.

God gave to [the African Hebrews] instruction in all the principles essential to physical as well as to moral health, and it was concerning these principles no less than concerning those of the moral law that He commanded them:

"These words, which I command thee this day, shall be in thine heart: and thou shalt teach them diligently unto thy children, and shalt talk of them when thou sittest in thine house, and when thou walkest by the way, and when thou liest down, and when thou risest up. And thou shalt bind them for a sign upon thine hand, and they shall be as frontlets between thine eyes. And thou shalt write them upon the posts of thy house, and on thy gates." Deuteronomy 6:6-9.

"And when thy son asketh thee in time to come, saying, What mean the testimonies, and the statutes, and the judgments, which the Lord our God hath commanded you? Then thou shalt say unto thy son, . . . The Lord commanded us to do all these statutes, to fear the

Lord our God, for our good always, that He might preserve us alive, as it is at this day." Verses 20-24. See Deuteronomy 28:2-6; 28:18,19

"The Lord shall command the blessing upon thee in thy storehouses, and in all that thou settest thine hand unto; and He shall bless thee in the land which the Lord thy God giveth thee. The Lord shall establish thee an holy people unto Himself, as He hath sworn unto thee, if thou shalt keep the commandments of the Lord thy God, and walk in His ways. And all people of the earth shall see that thou art called by the name of the Lord; and they shall be afraid of thee. And the Lord shall make thee plenteous in goods, in the fruit of thy body, and in the fruit of thy cattle, and in the fruit of thy ground, in the land which the Lord sware unto thy fathers to give thee. The Lord shall open unto thee His good treasure, the heaven to give the rain unto thy land in his season, and to bless all the work of thine hand. . . And the Lord shall make thee the head, and not the tail; and thou shalt be above only, and thou shalt not be beneath; if that thou hearken unto the commandments of the Lord thy God, which I command thee this day, to observe and to do them." Verses 8-13 See Jeremiah 17:7; Psalm 92:1 14; 92:15, Leeser; Proverbs 3:1, 2, 23-26.

Had the [African Hebrews] obeyed the instruction they received, and profited by their advantages, they would have been the world's object lesson of health and prosperity. If as a people they had lived according to God's plan, they would have been preserved from the diseases that afflicted other nations. Above any other people they would have possessed physical strength and vigor of intellect. They would have been the mightiest nation on the earth. God said: "Thou shalt be blessed above all people." Deuteronomy 7:14.

CLOTHING & HEALTH

The Bible teaches modesty in dress. "In like manner also, that women adorn themselves in modest apparel." 1 Timothy 2:9. This forbids display in dress, gaudy colors, profuse ornamentation. Any device designed to attract attention to the wearer or to excite admiration, is excluded from the modest apparel which God's word enjoins.

Our dress is to be inexpensive–not with "gold, or pearls, or costly array." Verse 9.

Money is a trust from God. It is not ours to expend for the gratification of pride or ambition. In the hands of God's children it is food for the hungry, and clothing for the naked. It is a defense to the oppressed, a means of health to the sick, a means of preaching the gospel to the poor. You could bring happiness to many hearts by using wisely the means that is now spent for show. Consider the life of Christ. Study His character, and be partakers with Him in His self-denial.

In the professed Christian world enough is expended for jewels and needlessly expensive dress to feed all the hungry and to clothe the naked. Fashion and display absorb the means that might comfort the poor and the suffering. They rob the world of the gospel of the Saviour's love. Missions languish. Multitudes perish for want of Christian teaching. Beside our own doors and in foreign lands the heathen are untaught and unsaved. While God has laden the earth with His bounties and filled its storehouses with the comforts of life, while He has so freely given to us a saving knowledge of His truth, what excuse can we offer for permitting the cries of the widow and the fatherless, the sick and the suffering, the untaught and the unsaved, to ascend to heaven? In the day of God, when brought face to face with Him who gave His life for these needy ones, what excuse will those offer who are spending their time and money upon indulgences that God has forbidden? To such will not Christ say, "I was anhungered, and ye gave Me no meat: I was thirsty, and ye gave Me no drink: . . .naked, and ye clothed Me not: sick, and in prison, and ye visited Me not"? Matthew 25:42, 43.

But our clothing, while modest and simple, should be of good quality, of becoming colors, and suited for service. It should be chosen for durability rather than display. It should provide warmth and proper protection. The wise woman described in the Proverbs "is not afraid of the snow for her household: for all her household are clothed with double garments." Proverbs 31:21, margin.

Our dress should be cleanly. Uncleanliness in dress is unhealthful, and thus defiling to the body and to the soul. "Ye are the temple of God. . . .If any man defile the temple of God, him shall God destroy." 1 Corinthians 3:16, 17.

In all respects the dress should be healthful. "Above all things," God desires us to "be in health"–health of body and of soul. And we are to be workers together with Him for the health of both soul and body. Both are promoted by healthful dress.

It should have the grace, the beauty, the appropriateness of natural simplicity. Christ has warned us against the pride of life, but not against its grace and natural beauty. He pointed to the flowers of the field, to the lily unfolding in its purity, and said, "Even Solomon in all his glory was not arrayed like one of these." Matthew 6:29. Thus by the things of nature Christ illustrates the beauty that heaven values, the modest grace, the simplicity, the purity, the appropriateness, that would make our attire pleasing to Him.

The most beautiful dress He bids us wear upon the soul. No outward adorning can compare in value or loveliness with that "meek and quiet spirit" which in His sight is "of great price." 1 Peter 3:4.

To those who make the Saviour's principles their guide, how precious His words of promise:

"Why are ye anxious concerning raiment? . . . If God doth so clothe the grass of the field, which today is, and tomorrow is cast into the oven, shall He not much more clothe you? . . . Be not therefore anxious, saying, . . . Wherewithal shall we be clothed? . . . For your heavenly Father knoweth that ye have need of all these things. But seek ye first His kingdom, and His righteousness; and all these things shall be added unto you." Matthew 6:28-33, R.V.

"Thou wilt keep him in perfect peace, whose mind is stayed on Thee: because he trusteth in Thee." Isaiah 26:3.

What a contrast is this to the weariness, the unrest, the disease and wretchedness, that result from the rule of fashion! How contrary to the principles given in the Scriptures are many of the modes of dress that fashion prescribes! Think of the styles that have prevailed for the last few hundreds of years or even for the last few decades. How many of them, when not in fashion, would be declared immodest; how many would be pronounced inappropriate for a refined, God-fearing, self-respecting woman.

The making of changes in apparel for the sake of fashion merely is not sanctioned by the word of God. Changing styles and elaborate, costly ornamentation squander the time and means of the rich, and lay waste the energies of mind and soul. They impose a heavy burden on the middle and poorer classes. Many who can hardly earn a livelihood, and who with simple modes might make their own clothing, are compelled to resort to the dressmaker in order to be in fashion. Many a poor girl, for the sake of a stylish gown, has deprived herself of warm underwear, and paid the penalty with her life. Many another, coveting the display and elegance of the rich, has been enticed into paths of dishonesty and shame. Many a home is deprived of comforts, many a man is driven to embezzlement or bankruptcy, to satisfy the extravagant demands of the wife or children.

Many a woman, forced to prepare for herself or her children the stylish costumes demanded by fashion, is doomed to ceaseless drudgery. Many a mother with throbbing nerves and trembling fingers toils far into the night to add to her children's clothing ornamentation that contributes nothing to healthfulness, comfort, or real beauty. For the sake of fashion she sacrifices health and that calmness of spirit so essential to the right guidance of her children. The culture of mind and heart is neglected. The soul is dwarfed.

The mother has no time to study the principles of physical development, that she may know how to care for the health of her children. She has no time for ministering to their mental or spiritual needs, no time to sympathize with them in their little disappointments and trials, or to share in their interests and pursuits.

Almost as soon as they come into the world the children are subjected to fashion's influence. They hear more of dress than of their Saviour. They see their mothers consulting the fashion plates more earnestly than the Bible. The display of dress is treated as of greater importance than the development of character. Parents and children are robbed of that which is best and sweetest and truest in life. For fashion's sake they are cheated out of a preparation for the life to come.

It was the adversary of all good who instigated the invention of the ever-changing fashions. He desires nothing so much as to bring grief and dishonor to God by working the misery and ruin of human beings. One of the means by which he most effectually accomplishes this is the devices of fashion that weaken the body as well as enfeeble the mind and belittle the soul.

Women are subject to serious maladies, and their sufferings are greatly increased by their manner of dress. Instead of preserving their health for the trying emergencies that are sure to come, they by their wrong habits too often sacrifice not only health but life, and leave to their children a legacy of woe in a ruined constitution, perverted habits, and false ideas of life.

One of fashion's wasteful and mischievous devices is the skirt that sweeps the ground. Uncleanly, uncomfortable, inconvenient, unhealthful–all this and more is true of the trailing skirt. It is extravagant, both because of the superfluous material required and because of the needless wear on account of its length. And whoever has seen a woman in a trailing skirt, with hands filled with parcels, attempt to go up or down stairs, to enter a streetcar, to walk through a crowd, to walk in the rain or on a muddy road, needs no other proof of its inconvenience and discomfort.

Another serious evil is the wearing of skirts so that their weight must be sustained by the hips. This heavy weight, pressing upon the internal organs, drags them downward and causes weakness of the stomach and a feeling of lassitude, inclining the wearer to stoop, which further cramps the lungs, making correct breathing more difficult.

Of late years the dangers resulting from compression of the waist have been so fully discussed that few can be ignorant in regard to them; yet so great is the power of fashion that the evil continues. By this practice, women and young girls are doing themselves untold harm. It is essential to health that the chest have room to expand to its fullest extent in order that the lungs may be enabled to take full inspiration. When the lungs are restricted, the quantity of oxygen received into them is lessened. The blood is not properly vitalized, and the waste, poisonous matter which should be thrown off through the lungs is retained. In addition to this the circulation is hindered, and the internal organs are so cramped and crowded out of place that they cannot perform their work properly.

Tight lacing does not improve the form. One of the chief elements in physical beauty is symmetry, the harmonious proportion of parts. And the correct model for physical development is to be found, not in the figures displayed by French modistes, but in the human form as developed according to the laws of God in nature. God is the author of all beauty, and only as we conform to His ideal shall we approach the standard of true beauty.

Another evil which custom fosters is the unequal distribution of the clothing, so that while some parts of the body have more than is required, others are insufficiently clad. The feet and limbs, being remote from the vital organs, should be especially guarded from cold by abundant clothing. It is impossible to have health when the extremities are habitually cold; for if there is too little blood in them there will be too much in other portions of the body. Perfect health requires a perfect circulation; but this cannot be had while three or four times as much clothing is worn upon the body, where the vital organs are situated, as upon the feet and limbs.

A multitude of women are nervous and careworn because they deprive themselves of the pure air that would make pure blood, and of the freedom of motion that would send the blood bounding through the veins, giving life, health, and energy. Many women have become confirmed invalids when they might have enjoyed health, and many have died of consumption and other diseases when they might have lived their allotted term of life had they dressed in accordance with health principles and exercised freely in the open air.

In order to secure the most healthful clothing, the needs of every part of the body must be carefully studied. The character of the climate, the surroundings, the condition of health, the age, and the occupation must all be considered. Every article of dress should fit easily, obstructing neither the circulation of the blood nor a free, full, natural respiration. Everything worn should be so loose that when the arms are raised the clothing will be correspondingly lifted.

Women who are in failing health can do much for themselves by sensible dressing and exercise. When suitably dressed for outdoor enjoyment, let them exercise in the open air, carefully at first, but increasing the amount of exercise as they can endure it. By taking this course, many might regain health and live to take their share in the world's work.

INDEPENDENT OF FASHION

Let women themselves, instead of struggling to meet the demands of fashion, have the courage to dress healthfully and simply. Instead of sinking into a mere household drudge, let the wife and mother take time to read, to keep herself well informed, to be a companion to her husband, and to keep in touch with the developing minds of her children. Let her use wisely the opportunities now hers to influence her dear ones for the higher life. Let her take time to make the dear Saviour a daily companion and familiar friend. Let her take time for the study of His word, take time to go with the children into the fields, and learn of God through the beauty of His works.

Let her keep cheerful and buoyant. Instead of spending every moment in endless sewing, make the evening a pleasant social season, a family reunion after the day's duties. Many a man would thus be led to choose the society of his home before that of the clubhouse or the saloon. Many a boy would be kept from the street or the corner grocery. Many a girl would be saved from frivolous, misleading associations. The influence of the home would be to parents and children what God designed it should be, a lifelong blessing.

DIET AND HEALTH

Our bodies are built up from the food we eat. There is a constant breaking down of the tissues of the body; every movement of every organ involves waste, and this waste is repaired from our food. Each organ of the body requires its share of nutrition. The brain must be supplied with its portion; the bones, muscles, and nerves demand theirs. It is a wonderful process that transforms the food into blood and uses this blood to build up the varied parts of the body; but this process is going on continually, supplying with life and strength each nerve, muscle, and tissue.

SELECTION OF FOOD

Those foods should be chosen that best supply the elements needed for building up the body. In this choice, appetite is not a safe guide. Through wrong habits of eating, the appetite has become perverted. Often it demands food that impairs health and causes weakness instead of strength. We cannot safely be guided by the customs of society. The disease and suffering that everywhere prevail are largely due to popular errors in regard to diet.

In order to know what are the best foods, we must study God's original plan for man's diet. He who created man and who understands his needs appointed Adam his food. "Behold," He said, "I have given you every herb yielding seed, . . . and every tree, in which is the fruit of a tree yielding seed; to you it shall be for food." Genesis 1:29, A.R.V. Upon leaving Eden to gain his livelihood by tilling the earth under the curse of sin, man received permission to eat also "the herb of the field." Genesis 3:18.

Grains, fruits, nuts, and vegetables constitute the diet chosen for us by our Creator. These foods, prepared in as simple and natural a manner as possible, are the most healthful and nourishing. They impart a strength, a power of endurance, and a vigor of intellect that are not afforded by a more complex and stimulating diet.

But not all foods wholesome in themselves are equally suited to our needs under all circumstances. Care should be taken in the selection of food. Our diet should be suited to the season, to the climate in which we live, and to the occupation we follow. Some foods that are adapted for use at one season or in one climate are not suited to another. So there are different foods best suited for persons in different occupations. Often food that can be used with benefit by those engaged in hard physical labor is unsuitable for persons of sedentary pursuits or intense mental application. God has given us an ample variety of healthful foods, and each person should choose from it the things that experience and sound judgment prove to be best suited to his own necessities.

Nature's abundant supply of fruits, nuts, and grains is ample, and year by year the products of all lands are more generally distributed to all, by the increased facilities for transportation. As a result many articles of food which a few years ago were regarded as expensive luxuries are now within the reach of all as foods for everyday use. This is especially the case with dried and canned fruits.

Nuts and nut foods are coming largely into use to take the place of flesh meats. With nuts may be combined grains, fruits, and some roots, to make foods that are healthful and nourishing. Care should be taken, however, not to use too large a proportion of nuts. Those who realize ill effects from the use of nut foods may find the difficulty removed by attending to this precaution. It should be remembered, too, that some nuts are not so wholesome as others. Almonds are preferable to peanuts, but peanuts in limited quantities, used in connection with grains, are nourishing and digestible.

When properly prepared, olives, like nuts, supply the place of butter and flesh meats. The oil, as eaten in the olive, is far preferable to animal oil or fat. It serves as a laxative. Its use will be found beneficial to consumptives, and it is healing to an inflamed, irritated stomach.

Persons who have accustomed themselves to a rich, highly stimulating diet have an unnatural taste, and they cannot at once relish food that is plain and simple. It will take time for the taste to become natural and for the stomach to recover from the abuse it has suffered. But those who persevere in the use of wholesome food will, after a time, find it palatable. Its delicate and delicious flavors will be appreciated, and it will be eaten with greater enjoyment than can be derived from unwholesome dainties. And the stomach, in a healthy condition, neither fevered nor overtaxed, can readily perform its task.

In order to maintain health, a sufficient supply of good, nourishing food is needed.

If we plan wisely, that which is most conducive to health can be secured in almost every land. The various preparations of rice, wheat, corn, and oats are sent abroad everywhere, also beans, peas, and lentils. These, with native or imported fruits, and the variety of vegetables that grow in each locality, give an opportunity to select a dietary that is complete without the use of flesh meats.

Wherever fruit can be grown in abundance, a liberal supply should be prepared for winter, by canning or drying. Small fruits, such as currants, gooseberries, strawberries, raspberries, and blackberries, can be grown to advantage in many places where they are but little used and their cultivation is neglected.

For household canning, glass, rather than tin cans, should be used whenever possible. It is especially necessary that the fruit for canning should be in good condition. Use little sugar, and cook the fruit only long enough to ensure its preservation. Thus prepared, it is an excellent substitute for fresh fruit.

Wherever dried fruits, such as raisins, prunes, apples, pears, peaches, and apricots are obtainable at moderate prices, it will be found that they can be used as staple articles of diet much more freely than is customary, with the best results to the health and vigor of all classes of workers.

There should not be a great variety at any one meal, for this encourages overeating and causes indigestion.

It is not well to eat fruit and vegetables at the same meal. If the digestion is feeble, the use of both will often cause distress and inability to put forth mental effort. It is better to have the fruit at one meal and the vegetables at another.

The meals should be varied. The same dishes, prepared in the same way, should not appear on the table meal after meal and day after day. The meals are eaten with greater relish, and the system is better nourished, when the food is varied.

PREPARATION OF FOOD

It is wrong to eat merely to gratify the appetite, but no indifference should be manifested regarding the quality of the food or the manner of its preparation. If the food eaten is not relished, the body will not be so well nourished. The food should be carefully chosen and prepared with intelligence and skill.

For use in breadmaking, the superfine white flour is not the best. Its use is neither healthful nor economical. Fine-flour bread is lacking in nutritive elements to be found in bread made from the whole wheat. It is a frequent cause of constipation and other unhealthful conditions.

The use of soda or baking powder in breadmaking is harmful and unnecessary. Soda causes inflammation of the stomach and often poisons the entire system. Many housewives think that they cannot make good bread without soda, but this is an error. If they would take the trouble to learn better methods, their bread would be more wholesome, and, to a natural taste, it would be more palatable.

In the making of raised or yeast bread, milk should not be used in place of water. The use of milk is an additional expense, and it makes the bread much less wholesome. Milk bread does not keep sweet so long after baking as does that made with water, and it ferments more readily in the stomach.

Bread should be light and sweet. Not the least taint of sourness should be tolerated. The loaves should be small and so thoroughly baked that, so far as possible, the yeast germs shall be destroyed. When hot or new, raised bread of any kind is difficult of digestion. It should never appear on the table. This rule does not, however, apply to unleavened bread. Fresh rolls made of wheaten meal without yeast or leaven, and baked in a well-heated oven, are both wholesome and palatable.

Grains used for porridge or "mush" should have several hours' cooking. But soft or liquid foods are less wholesome than dry foods, which require thorough mastication. Zwieback, or twice-baked break, is one of the most easily digested and most palatable of foods. Let ordinary raised bread be cut in slices and dried in a warm oven till the last trace of moisture disappears. Then let it be browned slightly all the way through. In a dry place this bread can be kept much longer than ordinary bread, and, if reheated before using, it will be as fresh as when new.

Far too much sugar is ordinarily used in food. Cakes, sweet puddings, pastries, jellies, jams, are active causes of indigestion. Especially harmful are the custards and puddings in which milk, eggs, and sugar are the chief ingredients. The free use of milk and sugar taken together should be avoided.

If milk is used, it should be thoroughly sterilized; with this precaution, there is less danger of contracting disease from its use. Butter is less harmful when eaten on cold bread than when used in cooking; but, as a rule, it is better to dispense with it altogether. Cheese is still more objectionable; it is wholly unfit for food. Scanty, ill-cooked food depraves the blood by weakening the blood-making organs. It deranges the system and brings on disease, with its accompaniment of irritable nerves and bad tempers. The victims of poor cookery are numbered by thousands and tens of thousands. Over many graves might be written: "Died because of poor cooking;" "Died of an abused stomach."

It is a sacred duty for those who cook to learn how to prepare healthful food. Many souls are lost as the result of poor cookery. It takes thought and care to make good bread; but there is more religion in a loaf of good bread than many think. There are few really good cooks. Young women think that it is menial to cook and do other kinds of housework, and for this reason many girls who marry and have the care of families have little idea of the duties devolving upon a wife and mother.

Cooking is no mean science, and it is one of the most essential in practical life. It is a science that all women should learn, and it should be taught in a way to benefit the poorer classes. To make food appetizing and at the same time simple and nourishing, requires skill; but it can be done. Cooks should know how to prepare simple food in a simple and healthful manner, and so that it will be found more palatable, as well as more wholesome, because of its simplicity.

Every woman who is at the head of a family and yet does not understand the art of healthful cookery should determine to learn that which is so essential to the well-being of her household. In many places hygienic cooking schools afford opportunity for instruction in this line. She who has not the help of such facilities should put herself under the instruction of some good cook and persevere in her efforts for improvement until she is mistress of the culinary art.

Regularity in eating is of vital importance. There should be a specified time for each meal. At this time let everyone eat what the system requires and then take nothing more until the next meal. There are many who eat when the system needs no food, at irregular intervals, and between meals, because they have not sufficient strength of will to resist inclination. When traveling, some are constantly nibbling if anything eatable is within their reach. This is very injurious. If travelers would eat regularly of food that is simple and nutritious, they would not feel so great weariness nor suffer so much from sickness.

Another pernicious habit is that of eating just before bedtime. The regular meals may have been taken; but because there is a sense of faintness, more food is eaten. By indulgence this wrong practice becomes a habit and often so firmly fixed that it is thought impossible to sleep without food. As a result of eating late suppers, the digestive process is continued through the sleeping hours. But though the stomach works constantly, its work is not properly accomplished. The sleep is often disturbed with unpleasant dreams, and in the morning the person awakes unrefreshed and with little relish for breakfast. When we lie down to rest, the stomach should have its work all done, that it, as well as the other organs of the body, may enjoy rest. For persons of sedentary habits, late suppers are particularly harmful. With them the disturbance created is often the beginning of disease that ends in death.

In many cases the faintness that leads to a desire for food is felt because the digestive organs have been too severely taxed during the day. After disposing of one meal, the digestive organs need rest. At least five or six hours should intervene between the meals, and most persons who give the plan a trial will find that two meals a day are better than three.

WRONG CONDITIONS OF EATING

Food should not be eaten very hot or very cold. If food is cold, the vital force of the stomach is drawn upon in order to warm it before digestion can take place. Cold drinks are injurious for the same reason; while the free use of hot drinks is debilitating. In fact, the more liquid there is taken with the meals, the more difficult it is for the food to digest; for the liquid must be absorbed before digestion can begin. Do not eat largely of salt, avoid the use of pickles and spiced foods, eat an abundance of fruit, and the irritation that calls for so much drink at mealtime will largely disappear.

Food should be eaten slowly and should be thoroughly masticated. This is necessary in order that the saliva may be properly mixed with the food and the digestive fluids be called into action.

Another serious evil is eating at improper times, as after violent or excessive exercise, when one is much exhausted or heated. Immediately after eating there is a strong draft upon the nervous energies; and when mind or body is heavily taxed just before or just after eating, digestion is hindered. When one is excited, anxious, or hurried, it is better not to eat until rest or relief is found.

The stomach is closely related to the brain; and when the stomach is diseased, the nerve power is called from the brain to the aid of the weakened digestive organs. When these demands are too frequent, the brain becomes congested. When the brain is constantly taxed, and there is lack of physical exercise, even plain food should be eaten sparingly. At mealtime cast off care and anxious thought; do not feel hurried, but eat slowly and with cheerfulness, with your heart filled with gratitude to God for all His blessings.

Many who discard flesh meats and other gross and injurious articles think that because their food is simple and wholesome they may indulge appetite without restraint, and they eat to excess, sometimes to gluttony. This is an error. The digestive organs should not be burdened with a quantity or quality of food which it will tax the system to appropriate.

Custom has decreed that the food shall be placed upon the table in courses. Not knowing what is coming next, one may eat a sufficiency of food which perhaps is not the best suited to him. When the last course is brought on, he often ventures to overstep the bounds, and take the tempting dessert, which, however, proves anything but good for him. If all the food intended for a meal is placed on the table at the beginning, one has opportunity to make the best choice.

Sometimes the result of overeating is felt at once. In other cases there is no sensation of pain; but the digestive organs lose their vital force, and the foundation of physical strength is undermined.

The surplus food burdens the system and produces morbid,

feverish conditions. It calls an undue amount of blood to the stomach, causing the limbs and extremities to chill quickly. It lays a heavy tax on the digestive organs, and when these organs have accomplished their task, there is a feeling of faintness or languor. Some who are continually overeating call this all-gone feeling hunger; but it is caused by the over-worked condition of the digestive organs. At times there is numbness of the brain, with disinclination to mental or physical effort.

These unpleasant symptoms are felt because nature has accomplished her work at an unnecessary outlay of vital force and is thoroughly exhausted. The stomach is saying, "Give me rest." But with many the faintness is interpreted as a demand for more food; so instead of giving the stomach rest, another burden is placed upon it. As a consequence the digestive organs are often worn out when they should be capable of doing good work.

We should not provide for the Sabbath a more liberal supply or a greater variety of food than for other days. Instead of this the food should be more simple, and less should be eaten in order that the mind may be clear and vigorous to comprehend spiritual things. A clogged stomach means a clogged brain. The most precious words may be heard and not appreciated because the mind is confused by an improper diet. By overeating on the Sabbath, many do more than they think to unfit themselves for receiving the benefit of its sacred opportunities.

Cooking on the Sabbath should be avoided; but it is not therefore necessary to eat cold food. In cold weather the food prepared the day before should be heated. And let the meals, however simple, be palatable and attractive. Especially in families where there are children, it is well, on the Sabbath, to provide something that will be regarded as a treat, something the family do not have every day.

Where wrong habits of diet have been indulged, there should be no delay in reform. When dyspepsia has resulted from abuse of the stomach, efforts should be made carefully to preserve the remaining strength of the vital forces by removing every overtaxing burden. The stomach may never entirely recover health after long abuse; but a proper course of diet will save further debility, and many will recover more or less fully. It is not easy to prescribe rules that will meet every case; but, with attention to right principles in eating, great reforms may be made, and the cook need not be continually toiling to tempt the appetite.

Abstemiousness in diet is rewarded with mental and moral vigor; it also aids in the control of the passions. Overeating is especially harmful to those who are sluggish in temperament; these should eat sparingly and take plenty of physical exercise. There are men and women of excellent natural ability who do not accomplish half what they might if they would exercise self-control in the denial of appetite.

Many writers and speakers fail here. After eating heartily, they give themselves to sedentary occupations, reading, study, or writing, allowing no time for physical exercise. As a consequence the free flow of thought and words is checked. They cannot write or speak with the force and intensity necessary in order to reach the heart; their efforts are tame and fruitless.

Those upon whom rest important responsibilities, those, above all, who are guardians of spiritual interests, should be men of keen feeling and quick perception. More than others, they need to be temperate in eating. Rich and luxurious food should have no place upon their tables.

Every day men in positions of trust have decisions to make upon which depend results of great importance. Often they have to think rapidly, and this can be done successfully by those only who practice strict temperance. The mind strengthens under the correct treatment of the physical and mental powers. If the strain is not too great, new vigor comes with every taxation. But often the work of those who have important plans to consider and important decisions to make is affected for evil by the results of improper diet. A disordered stomach produces a disordered, uncertain state of mind. Often it causes irritability, harshness, or injustice. Many a plan that would have been a blessing to the world has been set aside, many unjust, oppressive, even cruel measures have been carried, as the result of diseased conditions due to wrong habits of eating.

Here is a suggestion for all whose work is sedentary or chiefly mental; let those who have sufficient moral courage and self-control try it: At each meal take only two or three kinds of simple food, and eat no more than is required to satisfy hunger. Take active exercise every day, and see if you do not receive benefit.

Strong men who are engaged in active physical labor are not

compelled to be as careful as to the quantity or quality of their food as are persons of sedentary habits; but even these would have better health if they would practice self-control in eating and drinking.

Some wish that an exact rule could be prescribed for their diet. They overeat, and then regret it, and so they keep thinking about what they eat and drink. This is not as it should be. One person cannot lay down an exact rule for another. Everyone should exercise reason and self-control, and should act from principle.

Our bodies are Christ's purchased possession, and we are not at liberty to do with them as we please. All who understand the laws of health should realize their obligation to obey these laws which God has established in their being. Obedience to the laws of health is to be made a matter of personal duty. We ourselves must suffer the results of violated law. We must individually answer to God for our habits and practices. Therefore the question with us is not, "What is the world's practice?" but, "How shall I as an individual treat the habitation that God has given me?"

FAMILY LIFE AND HEALTH

What the parents are, that, to a great extent, the children will be. The physical conditions of the parents, their dispositions and appetites, their mental and moral tendencies, are, to a greater or less degree, reproduced in their children.

The nobler the aims, the higher the mental and spiritual endowments, and the better developed the physical powers of the parents, the better will be the life equipment they give their children. In cultivating that which is best in themselves, parents are exerting an influence to mold society and to uplift future generations.

Fathers and mothers need to understand their responsibility. The world is full of snares for the feet of the young. Multitudes are attracted by a life of selfish and sensual pleasure. They cannot discern the hidden dangers or the fearful ending of the path that seems to them the way of happiness. Through the indulgence of appetite and passion, their energies are wasted, and millions are ruined for this world and for the world to come. Parents should remember that their children must encounter these temptations. Even before the birth of the child, the preparation should begin that will enable it to fight successfully the battle against evil.

Especially does responsibility rest upon the mother. She, by whose lifeblood the child is nourished and its physical frame built up, imparts to it also mental and spiritual influences that tend to the shaping of mind and character. It was Jochebed, the Hebrew mother, who, strong in faith, was "not afraid of the king's commandment" (Hebrews 11:23), of whom was born Moses, the deliverer of Israel. It was Hannah, the woman of prayer and self-sacrifice and heavenly inspiration, who gave birth to Samuel, the heaven-instructed child, the incorruptible judge, the founder of Israel's sacred schools. It was Elizabeth the kinswoman and kindred spirit of Mary of Nazareth, who was the mother of the Saviour's herald.

TEMPERANCE AND SELF-CONTROL

The carefulness with which the mother should guard her habits of life is taught in the Scriptures. When the Lord would raise up Samson as a deliverer for Israel, "the angel of Jehovah" appeared to the mother, with special instruction concerning her habits, and also for the treatment of her child. "Beware," he said, "and now drink no wine nor strong drink, neither eat any unclean thing." Judges 13:13, 7.

The effect of prenatal influences is by many parents looked upon as a matter of little moment; but heaven does not so regard it. The message sent by an angel of God, and twice given in the most solemn manner, shows it to be deserving of our most careful thought.

In the words spoken to the Hebrew mother, God speaks to all mothers in every age. "Let her beware," the angel said; "all that I commanded her let her observe." The well-being of the child will be affected by the habits of the mother. Her appetites and passions are to be controlled by principle. There is something for her to shun, something for her to work against, if she fulfills God's purpose for her in giving her a child. If before the birth of her child she is self-indulgent, if she is selfish, impatient, and exacting, these traits will be reflected in the disposition of the child. Thus many children have received as a birthright almost unconquerable tendencies to evil.

But if the mother unswervingly adheres to right principles, if she is temperate and self-denying, if she is kind, gentle, and unselfish, she may give her child these same precious traits of character. Very explicit was the command prohibiting the use of wine by the mother. Every drop of strong drink taken by her to gratify appetite endangers the physical, mental, and moral health of her child, and is a direct sin against her Creator.

Many advisers urge that every wish of the mother should be gratified; that if she desires any article of food, however harmful, she should freely indulge her appetite. Such advice is false and mischievous. The mother's physical needs should in no case be neglected. Two lives are depending upon her, and her wishes should be tenderly regarded, her needs generously supplied. But at this time above all others she should avoid, in diet and in every other line, whatever would lessen physical or mental strength. By the command of God Himself she is placed under the most solemn obligation to exercise self-control.

OVERWORK

The strength of the mother should be tenderly cherished. Instead of spending her precious strength in exhausting labor, her care and burdens should be lessened. Often the husband and father is unacquainted with the physical laws which the well-being of his family requires him to understand. Absorbed in the struggle for a livelihood, or bent on acquiring wealth and pressed with cares and perplexities, he allows to rest upon the wife and mother burdens that overtax her strength at the most critical period and cause feebleness and disease.

Many a husband and father might learn a helpful lesson from the carefulness of the faithful shepherd. Jacob, when urged to undertake a rapid and difficult journey, made answer:

"The children are tender, and the flocks and herds with young are with me: and if men should overdrive them one day, all the flock will die. . . . I will lead on softly, according as the cattle that goeth before me and the children be able to endure." Genesis 33:13, 14.

In life's toilsome way let the husband and father "lead on softly," as the companion of his journey is able to endure. Amidst the world's eager rush for wealth and power, let him learn to stay his steps, to comfort and support the one who is called to walk by his side.

CHEERFULNESS

The mother should cultivate a cheerful, contented, happy disposition. Every effort in this direction will be abundantly repaid in both the physical well-being and the moral character of her children. A cheerful spirit will promote the happiness of her family and in a very great degree improve her own health.

Let the husband aid his wife by his sympathy and unfailing affection. If he wishes to keep her fresh and gladsome, so that she will be as sunshine in the home, let him help her bear her burdens. His kindness and loving courtesy will be to her a precious encouragement, and the happiness he imparts will bring joy and peace to his own heart.

The husband and father who is morose, selfish, and overbearing, is not only unhappy himself, but he casts gloom upon all the inmates of his home. He will reap the result in seeing his wife dispirited and sickly, and his children marred with his own unlovely temper.

If the mother is deprived of the care and comforts she should have, if she is allowed to exhaust her strength through overwork or through anxiety and gloom, her children will be robbed of the vital force and of the mental elasticity and cheerful buoyancy they should inherit. Far better will it be to make the mother's life bright and cheerful, to shield her from want, wearing labor, and depressing care, and let the children inherit good constitutions, so that they may battle their way through life with their own energetic strength.

Great is the honor and the responsibility placed upon fathers and mothers, in that they are to stand in the place of God to their children. Their character, their daily life, their methods of training, will interpret His words to the little ones. Their influence will win or repel the child's confidence in the Lord's assurances.

THE PRIVILEGE OF PARENTS IN CHILD TRAINING

Happy are the parents whose lives are a true reflection of the divine, so that the promises and commands of God awaken in the child gratitude and reverence; the parents whose tenderness and justice and long-suffering interpret to the child the love and justice and long-suffering of God; and who, by teaching the child to love and trust and obey them, are teaching him to love and trust and obey his Father in heaven. Parents who impart to a child such a gift have endowed him with a treasure more precious than the wealth of all the ages–a treasure as enduring as eternity.

In the children committed to her care, every mother has a sacred charge from God. "Take this son, this daughter," He says; "train it for Me; give it a character polished after the similitude of a palace, that it may shine in the courts of the Lord forever."

The mother's work often seems to her an unimportant service. It is a work that is rarely appreciated. Others know little of her many cares and burdens. Her days are occupied with a round of little duties, all calling for patient effort, for self-control, for tact, wisdom, and self-sacrificing love; yet she cannot boast of what she has done as any great achievement. She has only kept things in the home running smoothly; often weary and perplexed, she has tried to speak kindly to the children, to keep them busy and happy, and to guide the little feet in the right path. She feels that she has accomplished nothing. But it is not so. Heavenly angels watch the care-worn mother, noting the burdens she carries day by day. Her name may not have been heard in the world, but it is written in the Lamb's book of life.

THE MOTHER'S OPPORTUNITY

There is a God above, and the light and glory from His throne rests upon the faithful mother as she tries to educate her children to resist the influence of evil. No other work can equal hers in importance. She has not, like the artist, to paint a form of beauty upon canvas, nor, like the sculptor, to chisel it from marble. She has not, like the author, to embody a noble thought in words of power, nor, like the musician, to express a beautiful sentiment in melody. It is hers, with the help of God, to develop in a human soul the likeness of the divine.

The mother who appreciates this will regard her opportunities as priceless. Earnestly will she seek, in her own character and by her methods of training, to present before her children the highest ideal. Earnestly, patiently, courageously, she will endeavor to improve her own abilities, that she may use aright the highest powers of the mind in the training of her children. Earnestly will she inquire at every step, "What hath God spoken?" Diligently she will study His word. She will keep her eyes fixed upon Christ, that her own daily experience, in the lowly round of care and duty, may be a true reflection of the one true Life.

THE CHILD

Not only the habits of the mother, but the training of the child were included in the angel's instruction to the Hebrew parents. It was not enough that Samson, the child who was to deliver Israel, should have a good legacy at his birth. This was to be followed by careful training. From infancy he was to be trained to habits of strict temperance.

Similar instruction was given in regard to John the Baptist. Before the birth of the child, the message sent from heaven to the father was:

"Thou shalt have joy and gladness; and many shall rejoice at his birth. For he shall be great in the sight of the Lord, and he shall drink no wine nor strong drink; and he shall be filled with the Holy Spirit." Luke 1:14, 15, A.R.V.

On heaven's record of noble men the Saviour declared that there stood not one greater than John the Baptist. The work committed to him was one demanding not only physical energy and endurance, but the highest qualities of mind and soul. So important was right physical training as a preparation for this work that the highest angel in heaven was sent with a message of instruction to the parents of the child.

The directions given concerning the Hebrew children teach us that nothing which affects the child's physical well-being is to be neglected. Nothing is unimportant. Every influence that affects the health of the body has its bearing upon mind and character.

Too much importance cannot be placed upon the early training of children. The lessons learned, the habits formed, during the years of infancy and childhood, have more to do with the formation of the character and the direction of the life than have all the instruction and training of after years.

Parents need to consider this. They should understand the principles that underlie the care and training of children. They should be capable of rearing them in physical, mental, and moral health. Parents should study the laws of nature. They should become acquainted with the organism of the human body. They need to understand the functions of the various organs, and their relation and dependence. They should study the relation of the mental to the physical powers, and the conditions required for the healthy action of each. To assume the responsibilities of parenthood without such preparation is a sin.

Far too little thought is given to the causes underlying the mortality, the disease and degeneracy, that exist today even in the most civilized and favored lands. The human race is deteriorating. More than one third die in infancy;*of those who reach manhood and womanhood, by far the greater number suffer from disease in some form, and but few reach the limit of human life. *[*The statement concerning infant mortality was correct at the time it was written in 1906.–Publishers*]

Most of the evils that are bringing misery and ruin to the race might be prevented, and the power to deal with them rests to a great degree with parents. It is not a "mysterious providence" that removes the little children. God does not desire their death. He gives them to the parents to be trained for usefulness here, and for heaven hereafter. Did fathers and mothers do what they might to give their children a good inheritance, and then by right management endeavor to remedy any wrong conditions of their birth, what a change for the better the world might see!

THE CARE OF INFANTS

The more quiet and simple the life of the child, the more favorable it will be to both physical and mental development. At all times the mother should endeavor to be quiet, calm, and self-possessed. Many infants are extremely susceptible to nervous excitement, and the mother's gentle, unhurried manner will have a soothing influence that will be of untold benefit to the child.

Babies require warmth, but a serious error is often committed in keeping them in overheated rooms, deprived to a great degree of fresh air. The practice of covering the infant's face while sleeping is harmful, since it prevents free respiration.

The baby should be kept free from every influence that would tend to weaken or to poison the system. The most scrupulous care should be taken to have everything about it sweet and clean. While it may be necessary to protect the little ones from sudden or too great changes of temperature, care should be taken, that, sleeping or waking, day or night, they breathe a pure, invigorating atmosphere.

In the preparation of the baby's wardrobe, convenience, comfort, and health should be sought before fashion or a desire to excite admiration. The mother should not spend time in embroidery and fancywork to make the little garments beautiful, thus taxing herself with unnecessary labor at the expense of her own health and the health of her child. She should not bend over sewing that severely taxes eyes and nerves, at a time when she needs much rest and pleasant exercise. She should realize her obligation to cherish her strength, that she may be able to meet the demands that will be made upon her.

If the dress of the child combines warmth, protection, and comfort, one of the chief causes of irritation and restlessness will be removed. The little one will have better health, and the mother will not find the care of the child so heavy a tax upon her strength and time.

Tight bands or waists hinder the action of the heart and lungs, and should be avoided. No part of the body should at any time be made uncomfortable by clothing that compresses any organ or restricts its freedom of movement. The clothing of all children should be loose enough to admit of the freest and fullest respiration, and so arranged that the shoulders will support its weight.

In some countries the custom of leaving bare the shoulders and limbs of little children still prevails. This custom cannot be too severely condemned. The limbs being remote from the center of circulation, demand greater protection than the other parts of the body. The arteries that convey the blood to the extremities are large, providing for a sufficient quantity of blood to afford warmth and nutrition. But when the limbs are left unprotected or are insufficiently clad, the arteries and veins become contracted, the sensitive portions of the body are chilled, and the circulation of the blood hindered.

In growing children all the forces of nature need every advantage to enable them to perfect the physical frame. If the limbs are insufficiently protected, children, and especially girls, cannot be out of doors unless the weather is mild. So they are kept in for fear of the cold. If children are well clothed, it will benefit them to exercise freely in the open air, summer or winter.

Mothers who desire their boys and girls to possess the vigor of health should dress them properly and encourage them in all reasonable weather to be much in the open air. It may require effort to break away from the chains of custom, and dress and educate the children with reference to health; but the result will amply repay the effort.

THE CHILD'S DIET

The best food for the infant is the food that nature provides. Of this it should not be needlessly deprived. It is a heartless thing for a mother, for the sake of convenience or social enjoyment, to seek to free herself from the tender office of nursing her little one.

The mother who permits her child to be nourished by another should consider well what the result may be. To a greater or less degree the nurse imparts her own temper and temperament to the nursing child.

The importance of training children to right dietetic habits can hardly be overestimated. The little ones need to learn that they eat to live, not live to eat. The training should begin with the infant in its mother's arms. The child should be given food only at regular intervals, and less frequently as it grows older. It should not be given sweets, or the food of older persons, which it is unable to digest. Care and regularity in the feeding of infants will not only promote health, and thus tend to make them quiet and sweet-tempered, but will lay the foundation of habits that will be a blessing to them in after years.

As children emerge from babyhood, great care should still be taken in educating their tastes and appetite. Often they are permitted to eat what they choose and when they choose, without reference to health. The pains and money so often lavished upon unwholesome dainties lead the young to think that the highest object in life, and that which yields the greatest amount of happiness, is to be able to indulge the appetite. The result of this training is gluttony, then comes sickness, which is usually followed by dosing with poisonous drugs.

Parents should train the appetites of their children and should not permit the use of unwholesome foods. But in the effort to regulate the diet, we should be careful not to err in requiring children to eat that which is distasteful, or to eat more than is needed. Children have rights, they have preferences, and when these preferences are reasonable they should be respected.

Regularity in eating should be carefully observed. Nothing should be eaten between meals, no confectionery, nuts, fruits, or food of any kind. Irregularities in eating destroy the healthful tone of the digestive organs, to the detriment of health and cheerfulness. And when the children come to the table, they do not relish wholesome food; their appetites crave that which is hurtful for them.

Mothers who gratify the desires of their children at the expense of health and happy tempers, are sowing seeds of evil that will spring up and bear fruit. Self-indulgence grows with the growth of the little ones, and both mental and physical vigor are sacrificed. Mothers who do this work reap with bitterness the seed they have sown. They see their children grow up unfitted in mind and character to act a noble and useful part in society or in the home. The spiritual as well as the mental and physical powers suffer under the influence of unhealthful food. The conscience becomes stupefied, and the susceptibility to good impressions is impaired.

While the children should be taught to control the appetite and to eat with reference to health; let it be made plain that they are denying themselves only that which would do them harm. They give up hurtful things for something better. Let the table be made inviting and attractive, as it is supplied with the good things which God has so bountifully bestowed. Let mealtime be a cheerful, happy time. As we enjoy the gifts of God, let us respond by grateful praise to the Giver.

THE CARE OF CHILDREN IN SICKNESS

In many cases the sickness of children can be traced to errors in management. Irregularities in eating, insufficient clothing in the chilly evening, lack of vigorous exercise to keep the blood in healthy circulation, or lack of abundance of air for its purification, may be the cause of the trouble. Let the parents study to find the causes of the sickness, and then remedy the wrong conditions as soon as possible.

All parents have it in their power to learn much concerning the care and prevention, and even the treatment, of disease. Especially ought the mother to know what to do in common cases of illness in her family. She should know how to minister to her sick child. Her love and insight should fit her to perform services for it which could not so well be trusted to a stranger's hand.

THE STUDY OF PHYSIOLOGY

Parents should early seek to interest their children in the study of physiology and should teach them its simpler principles. Teach them how best to preserve the physical, mental, and spiritual powers, and how to use their gifts so that their lives may bring blessing to one another and honor to God. This knowledge is invaluable to the young. An education in the things that concern life and health is more important to them than a knowledge of many of the sciences taught in the schools.

Parents should live more for their children, and less for society. Study health subjects, and put your knowledge to a practical use. Teach your children to reason from cause to effect. Teach them that if they desire health and happiness, they must obey the laws of nature. Though you may not see so rapid improvement as you desire, be not discouraged, but patiently and perseveringly continue your work.

Teach your children from the cradle to practice self-denial and self-control. Teach them to enjoy the beauties of nature and in useful employments to exercise systematically all the powers of body and mind. Bring them up to have sound constitutions and good morals, to have sunny dispositions and sweet tempers. Impress upon their tender minds the truth that God does not design that we should live for present gratification merely, but for our ultimate good. Teach them that to yield to temptation is weak and wicked; to resist, noble and manly. These lessons will be as seed sown in good soil, and they will bear fruit that will make your hearts glad.

Above all things else, let parents surround their children with an atmosphere of cheerfulness, courtesy, and love. A home where love dwells, and where it is expressed in looks, in words, and in acts, is a place where angels delight to manifest their presence.

Parents, let the sunshine of love, cheerfulness, and happy contentment enter your own hearts, and let its sweet, cheering influence pervade your home. Manifest a kindly, forbearing spirit; and encourage the same in your children, cultivating all the graces that will brighten the home life. The atmosphere thus created will be to the children what air and sunshine are to the vegetable world, promoting health and vigor of mind and body.

HOME INFLUENCES

The home should be to the children the most attractive place in the world, and the mother's presence should be its greatest attraction. Children have sensitive, loving natures. They are easily pleased and easily made unhappy. By gentle discipline, in loving words and acts, mothers may bind their children to their hearts.

Young children love companionship and can seldom enjoy themselves alone. They yearn for sympathy and tenderness. That which they enjoy they think will please mother also, and it is natural for them to go to her with their little joys and sorrows. The mother should not wound their sensitive hearts by treating with indifference matters that, though trifling to her, are of great importance to them. Her sympathy and approval are precious. An approving glance, a word of encouragement or commendation, will be like sunshine in their hearts, often making the whole day happy.

Instead of sending her children from her, that she may not be annoyed by their noise or troubled by their little wants, let the mother plan amusement or light work to employ the active hands and minds.

By entering into their feelings and directing their amusements and employments, the mother will gain the confidence of her children, and she can the more effectually correct wrong habits, or check the manifestations of selfishness or passion. A word of caution or reproof spoken at the right time will be of great value. By patient, watchful love, she can turn the minds of the children in the right direction, cultivating in them beautiful and attractive traits of character.

Mothers should guard against training their children to be dependent and self-absorbed. Never lead them to think that they are the center, and that everything must revolve around them. Some parents give much time and attention to amusing their children, but children should be trained to amuse themselves, to exercise their own ingenuity and skill. Thus they will learn to be content with very simple pleasures. They should be taught to bear bravely their little disappointments and trials. Instead of calling attention to every trifling pain or hurt, divert their minds, teach them to pass lightly over little annoyances or discomforts. Study to suggest ways by which the children may learn to be thoughtful for others.

But let not the children be neglected. Burdened with many cares, mothers sometimes feel that they cannot take time patiently to instruct their little ones and give them love and sympathy. But they should remember that if the children do not find in their parents and in their home that which will satisfy their desire for sympathy and companionship, they will look to other sources, where both mind and character may be endangered.

For lack of time and thought, many a mother refuses her children some innocent pleasure, while busy fingers and weary eyes are diligently engaged on work designed only for adornment, something that, at best, will serve only to encourage vanity and extravagance in their young hearts. As the children approach manhood and womanhood, these lessons bear fruit in pride and moral worthlessness. The mother grieves over her children's faults, but does not realize that the harvest she is reaping is from seed which she herself planted.

Some mothers are not uniform in the treatment of their children. At times they indulge them to their injury, and again they refuse some innocent gratification that would make the childish heart very happy. In this they do not imitate Christ; He loved the children; He comprehended their feelings and sympathized with them in their pleasures and their trials.

THE FATHER'S RESPONSIBILITY

The husband and father is the head of the household. The wife looks to him for love and sympathy, and for aid in the training of the children; and this is right. The children are his as well as hers, and he is equally interested in their welfare. The children look to their father for support and guidance; he needs to have a right conception of life and of the influences and associations that should surround his family; above all, he should be controlled by the love and fear of God and by the teaching of His word, that he may guide the feet of his children in the right way.

The father is the lawmaker of the household; and, like Abraham, he should make the law of God the rule of his home. God said of Abraham, "I know him, that he will command his children and his household." Genesis 18:19. There would be no sinful neglect to restrain evil, no weak, unwise, indulgent favoritism; no yielding of his conviction of duty to the claims of mistaken affection. Abraham would not only give right instruction, but he would maintain the authority of just and righteous laws. God has given rules for our guidance. Children should not be left to wander away from the safe path marked out in God's word, into ways leading to danger, which are open on every side. Kindly, but firmly, with persevering, prayerful effort, their wrong desires should be restrained, their inclinations denied.

The father should enforce in his family the sterner virtues – energy, integrity, honesty, patience, courage, diligence, and practical usefulness. And what he requires of his children he himself should practice, illustrating these virtues in his own manly bearing.

But, fathers, do not discourage your children. Combine affection with authority, kindness and sympathy with firm restraint. Give some of your leisure hours to your children; become acquainted with them; associate with them in their work and in their sports, and win their confidence. Cultivate friendship with them, especially with your sons. In this way you will be a strong influence for good.

The father should do his part toward making home happy. Whatever his cares and business perplexities, they should not be permitted to overshadow his family; he should enter his home with smiles and pleasant words.

In a sense the father is the priest of the household, laying upon the family altar the morning and evening sacrifice. But the wife and children should unite in prayer and join in the song of praise. In the morning before he leaves home for his daily labor, let the father gather his children about him and, bowing before God, commit them to the care of the Father in heaven. When the cares of the day are past, let the family unite in offering grateful prayer and raising the song of praise, in acknowledgment of divine care during the day.

Fathers and mothers, however pressing your business, do not fail to gather your family around God's altar. Ask for the guardianship of holy angels in your home. Remember that your dear ones are exposed to temptations. Daily annoyances beset the path of young and old. Those who would live patient, loving, cheerful lives must pray. Only by receiving constant help from God can we gain the victory over self.

Home should be a place where cheerfulness, courtesy, and love abide; and where these graces dwell, there will abide happiness and peace. Troubles may invade, but these are the lot of humanity. Let patience, gratitude, and love keep sunshine in the heart, though the day may be ever so cloudy. In such homes angels of God abide.

Let the husband and wife study each other's happiness, never failing in the small courtesies and little kindly acts that cheer and brighten the life. Perfect confidence should exist between husband and wife. Together they should consider their responsibilities. Together they should work for the highest good of their children. Never should they in the presence of the children criticize each other's plans or question each other's judgment. Let the wife be careful not to make the husband's work for the children more difficult. Let the husband hold up the hands of his wife, giving her wise counsel and loving encouragement.

No barrier of coldness and reserve should be allowed to arise between parents and children. Let parents become acquainted with their children, seeking to understand their tastes and dispositions, entering into their feelings, and drawing out what is in their hearts.

Parents, let your children see that you love them and will do all in your power to make them happy. If you do so, your necessary restrictions will have far greater weight in their young minds. Rule your children with tenderness and compassion, remembering that "their angels do always behold the face of My Father which is in heaven." Matthew 18:10. If you desire the angels to do for your children the work given them of God, co-operate with them by doing your part.

Brought up under the wise and loving guidance of a true home, children will have no desire to wander away in search of pleasure and companionship. Evil will not attract them. The spirit that prevails in the home will mold their characters; they will form habits and principles that will be a strong defense against temptation when they shall leave the home shelter and take their place in the world.

Children as well as parents have important duties in the home. They should be taught that they are a part of the home firm. They are fed and clothed and loved and cared for, and they should respond to these many mercies by bearing their share of the home burdens and bringing all the happiness possible into the family of which they are members.

Children are sometimes tempted to chafe under restraint; but in afterlife they will bless their parents for the faithful care and strict watchfulness that guarded and guided them in their years of inexperience.

IN THE SICKROOM

Those who minister to the sick should understand the importance of careful attention to the laws of health. Nowhere is obedience to these laws more important than in the sickroom. Nowhere does so much depend upon faithfulness in little things on the part of the attendants. In cases of serious illness, a little neglect, a slight inattention to a patient's special needs or dangers, the manifestation of fear, excitement, or petulance, even a lack of sympathy, may turn the scale that is balancing life and death, and cause to go down to the grave a patient who otherwise might have recovered.

The efficiency of the nurse depends, to a great degree, upon physical vigor. The better the health, the better will she be able to endure the strain of attendance upon the sick, and the more successfully can she perform her duties. Those who care for the sick should give special attention to diet, cleanliness, fresh air, and exercise. Like carefulness on the part of the family will enable them also to endure the extra burdens brought upon them, and will help to prevent them from contracting disease.

Where the illness is serious, requiring the attendance of a nurse night and day, the work should be shared by at least two efficient nurses, so that each may have opportunity for rest and for exercise in the open air. This is especially important in cases where it is difficult to secure an abundance of fresh air in the sickroom. Through ignorance of the importance of fresh air, ventilation is sometimes restricted, and the lives of both patient and attendant are often in danger.

If proper precaution is observed, noncontagious diseases need not be taken by others. Let the habits be correct, and by cleanliness and proper ventilation keep the sickroom free from poisonous elements. Under such conditions, the sick are much more likely to recover, and in most cases neither attendants nor the members of the family will contract the disease.

SUNLIGHT, VENTILATION, AND TEMPERATURE

To afford the patient the most favorable conditions for recovery, the room he occupies should be large, light, and cheerful, with opportunity for thorough ventilation. The room in the house that best meets these requirements should be chosen as the sickroom. Many houses have no special provision for proper ventilation, and to secure it is difficult; but every possible effort should be made to arrange the sickroom so that a current of fresh air can pass through it night and day.

So far as possible an even temperature should be maintained in the sickroom. The thermometer should be consulted. Those who have the care of the sick, being often deprived of sleep or awakened in the night to attend to the patient, are liable to chilliness and are not good judges of a healthful temperature.

DIET

An important part of the nurse's duty is the care of the patient's diet. The patient should not be allowed to suffer or become unduly weakened through lack of nourishment, nor should the enfeebled digestive powers be overtaxed. Care should be taken so to prepare and serve the food that it will be palatable, but wise judgment should be used in adapting it to the needs of the patient, both in quantity and quality. In times of convalescence especially, when the appetite is keen, before the digestive organs have recovered strength, there is great danger of injury from errors in diet.

DUTIES OF ATTENDANTS

Nurses, and all who have to do with the sickroom, should be cheerful, calm, and self-possessed. All hurry, excitement, or confusion, should be avoided. Doors should be opened and shut with care, and the whole household be kept quiet. In cases of fever, special care is needed when the crisis comes and the fever is passing away. Then constant watching is often necessary. Ignorance, forgetfulness, and recklessness have caused the death of many who might have lived had they received proper care from judicious, thoughtful nurses.

VISITING THE SICK

It is misdirected kindness, a false idea of courtesy, that leads to much visiting of the sick. Those who are very ill should not have visitors. The excitement connected with receiving callers wearies the patient at a time when he is in the greatest need of quiet, undisturbed rest.

To a convalescent or a patient suffering from chronic disease, it is often a pleasure and a benefit to know that he is kindly remembered; but this assurance conveyed by a message of sympathy or by some little gift will often serve a better purpose than a personal visit, and without danger of harm.

HOSPITAL NURSING

In sanitariums and hospitals, where nurses are constantly associated with large numbers of sick people, it requires a decided effort to be always pleasant and cheerful, and to show thoughtful consideration in every word and act. In these institutions it is of the utmost importance that the nurses strive to do their work wisely and well. They need ever to remember that in the discharge of their daily duties they are serving the Lord Christ.

The sick need to have wise words spoken to them. Nurses should study the Bible daily, that they may be able to speak words that will enlighten and help the suffering. Angels of God are in the rooms where these suffering ones are being ministered to, and the atmosphere surrounding the soul of the one giving treatment should be pure and fragrant. Physicians and nurses are to cherish the principles of Christ. In their lives His virtues are to be seen. Then, by what they do and say, they will draw the sick to the Saviour.

The Christian nurse, while administering treatment for the restoration of health, will pleasantly and successfully draw the mind of the patient to Christ, the healer of the soul as well as of the body. The thoughts presented, here a little and there a little, will have their influence. The older nurses should lose no favorable opportunity of calling the attention of the sick to Christ. They should be ever ready to blend spiritual healing with physical healing.

In the kindest and tenderest manner nurses are to teach that he who would be healed must cease to transgress the law of God. He must cease to choose a life of sin. God cannot bless the one who continues to bring upon himself disease and suffering by a willful violation of the laws of heaven. But Christ, through the Holy Spirit, comes as a healing power to those who cease to do evil and learn to do well.

Those who have no love for God will work constantly against the best interests of soul and body. But those who awake to the importance of living in obedience to God in this present evil world will be willing to separate from every wrong habit. Gratitude and love will fill their hearts. They know that Christ is their friend. In many cases the realization that they have such a friend means more to the suffering ones in their recovery from sickness than the best treatment that can be given. But both lines of ministry are essential. They are to go hand in hand.

PRAYER FOR THE SICK

The Scripture says that "men ought always to pray, and not to faint" (Luke 18:1); and if ever there is a time when they feel their need of prayer, it is when strength fails and life itself seems slipping from their grasp. Often those who are in health forget the wonderful mercies continued to them day by day, year after year, and they render no tribute of praise to God for His benefits. But when sickness comes, God is remembered. When human strength fails, men feel their need of divine help. And never does our merciful God turn from the soul that in sincerity seeks Him for help. He is our refuge in sickness as in health.

"Like as a father pitieth his children,
So the Lord pitieth them that fear Him.
For He knoweth our frame;
He remembereth that we are dust."

Psalm 103:13, 14.

"Because of their transgression,
And because of their iniquities, [men] are afflicted.
Their soul abhorreth all manner of food;
And they draw near unto the gates of death."

Psalm 107:17, 18, A.R.V.

"Then they cry unto the Lord in their trouble,
And He saveth them out of their distresses.
He sendeth His word, and healeth them,
And delivereth them from their destructions."

Verses 19, 20, R.V.

God is just as willing to restore the sick to health now as when the Holy Spirit spoke these words through the psalmist. And Christ is the same compassionate physician now that He was during His earthly ministry. In Him there is healing balm for every disease, restoring power for every infirmity. His disciples in this time are to pray for the sick as verily as the disciples of old prayed. And recoveries will follow; for "the prayer of faith shall save the sick." We have the Holy Spirit's power, the calm assurance of faith, that can claim God's promises. The Lord's promise, "They shall lay hands on the sick, and they shall recover" (Mark 16:18), is just as trustworthy now as in the days of the apostles. It presents the privilege of God's children, and our faith should lay hold of all that it embraces. Christ's servants are the channel of His working, and through them He desires to exercise His healing power. It is our work to present the sick and suffering to God in the arms of our faith. We should teach them to believe in the Great Healer.

The Saviour would have us encourage the sick, the hopeless, the afflicted, to take hold upon His strength. Through faith and prayer the sickroom may be transformed into a Bethel. In word and deed, physicians and nurses may say, so plainly that it cannot be misunderstood, "God is in this place" to save, and not to destroy. Christ desires to manifest His presence in the sickroom, filling the hearts of physicians and nurses with the sweetness of His love. If the life of the attendants upon the sick is such that Christ can go with them to the bedside of the patient, there will come to him the conviction that the compassionate Saviour is present, and this conviction will itself do much for the healing of both the soul and the body.

And God hears prayer. Christ has said, "If ye shall ask anything in My name, I will do it." Again He says, "If any man serve Me, him will My Father honor." John 14:14; 12:26. If we live according to His word, every precious promise He has given will be fulfilled to us. We are undeserving of His mercy, but as we give ourselves to Him, He receives us. He will work for and through those who follow Him.

But only as we live in obedience to His word can we claim the fulfillment of His promises. The psalmist says,

"If I regard iniquity in my heart, the Lord will not hear me." Psalm 66:18. If we render to Him only a partial, halfhearted obedience, His promises will not be fulfilled to us.

In the word of God we have instruction relative to special prayer for the recovery of the sick. But the offering of such prayer is a most solemn act, and should not be entered upon without careful consideration. In many cases of prayer for the healing of the sick, that which is called faith is nothing less than presumption.

Many persons bring disease upon themselves by their self-indulgence. They have not lived in accordance with natural law or the principles of strict purity. Others have disregarded the laws of health in their habits of eating and drinking, dressing, or working. Often some form of vice is the cause of feebleness of mind or body. Should these persons gain the blessing of health, many of them would continue to pursue the same course of heedless transgression of God's natural and spiritual laws, reasoning that if God heals them in answer to prayer, they are at liberty to continue their unhealthful practices and to indulge perverted appetite without restraint. If God were to work a miracle in restoring these persons to health, He would be encouraging sin.

It is labor lost to teach people to look to God as a healer of their infirmities, unless they are taught also to lay aside unhealthful practices. In order to receive His blessing in answer to prayer, they must cease to do evil and learn to do well. Their surroundings must be sanitary, their habits of life correct. They must live in harmony with the law of God, both natural and spiritual.

CONFESSION OF SIN

To those who desire prayer for their restoration to health, it should be made plain that the violation of God's law, either natural or spiritual, is sin, and that in order for them to receive His blessing, sin must be confessed and forsaken.

The Scripture bids us, "Confess your faults one to another, and pray one for another, that ye may be healed." James 5:16. To the one asking for prayer, let thoughts like these be presented: "We cannot read the heart, or know the secrets of your life. These are known only to yourself and to God. If you repent of your sins, it is your duty to make confession of them." Sin of a private character is to be confessed to Christ, the only mediator between God and man. For "if any man sin, we have an advocate with the Father, Jesus Christ the righteous." 1 John 2:1. Every sin is an offense against God and is to be confessed to Him through Christ. Every open sin should be as openly confessed. Wrong done to a fellow being should be made right with the one who has been offended. If any who are seeking health have been guilty of evilspeaking, if they have sowed discord in the home, the neighborhood, or the church, and have stirred up alienation and dissension, if by any wrong practice they have led others into sin, these things should be confessed before God and before those who have been offended. "If we confess our sins, He is faithful and just to forgive us our sins, and to cleanse us from all unrighteousness." 1 John 1:9.

When wrongs have been righted, we may present the needs of the sick to the Lord in calm faith, as His Spirit may indicate. He knows each individual by name, and cares for each as if there were not another upon the earth for whom He gave His beloved Son. Because God's love is so great and so unfailing, the sick should be encouraged to trust in Him and be cheerful. To be anxious about themselves tends to cause weakness and disease. If they will rise above depression and gloom, their prospect of recovery will be better; for "the eye of the Lord is upon them" "that hope in His mercy." Psalm 33:18.

In prayer for the sick it should be remembered that "we know not what we should pray for as we ought." Romans 8:26. We do not know whether the blessing we desire will be best or not. Therefore our prayers should include this thought: "Lord, thou knowest every secret of the soul. Thou art acquainted with these persons. Jesus, their Advocate, gave His life for them. His love for them is greater than ours can possibly be. If, therefore, it is for Thy glory and the good of the afflicted ones, we ask, in the name of Jesus, that they may be restored to health. If it be not Thy will that they may be restored, we ask that Thy grace may comfort and Thy presence sustain them in their sufferings."

God knows the end from the beginning. He is acquainted with the hearts of all men. He reads every secret of the soul. He knows whether those for whom prayer is offered would or would not be able to endure the trials that would come upon them should they live. He knows whether their lives would be a blessing or a curse to themselves and to the world. This is one reason why, while presenting our petitions with earnestness, we should say, "Nevertheless not my will, but Thine, be done." Luke 22:42. Jesus added these words of submission to the wisdom and will of God when in the Garden of Gethsemane He pleaded, "O My Father, if it be possible, let this cup pass from Me." Matthew 26:39. And if they were appropriate for Him, the Son of God, how much more are they becoming on the lips of finite, erring mortals!

The consistent course is to commit our desires to our all-wise heavenly Father, and then, in perfect confidence, trust all to Him. We know that God hears us if we ask according to His will. But to press our petitions without a submissive spirit is not right; our prayers must take the form, not of command, but of intercession.

There are cases where God works decidedly by His divine power in the restoration of health. But not all the sick are healed. Many are laid away to sleep in Jesus. John on the Isle of Patmos was bidden to write:

"Blessed are the dead which die in the Lord from henceforth: Yea, saith the Spirit, that they may rest from their labors; and their works do follow them." Revelation 14:13. From this we see that if persons are not raised to health, they should not on this account be judged as wanting in faith.

We all desire immediate and direct answers to our prayers, and are tempted to become discouraged when the answer is delayed or comes in an unlooked-for form. But God is too wise and good to answer our prayers always at just the time and in just the manner we desire. He will do more and better for us than to accomplish all our wishes. And because we can trust His wisdom and love, we should not ask Him to concede to our will, but should seek to enter into and accomplish His purpose. Our desires and interests should be lost in His will. These experiences that test faith are for our benefit. By them it is made manifest whether our faith is true and sincere, resting on the word of God alone, or whether depending on circumstances, it is uncertain and changeable. Faith is strengthened by exercise. We must let patience have its perfect work, remembering that there are precious promises in the Scriptures for those who wait upon the Lord.

Not all understand these principles. Many who seek the Lord's healing mercy think that they must have a direct and immediate answer to their prayers or their faith is defective. For this reason, those who are weakened by disease need to be counseled wisely, that they may act with discretion. They should not disregard their duty to the friends who may survive them, or neglect to employ nature's agencies for the restoration of health.

Often there is danger of error here. Believing that they will be healed in answer to prayer, some fear to do anything that might seem to indicate a lack of faith. But they should not neglect to set their affairs in order as they would desire to do if they expected to be removed by death. Nor should they fear to utter words of encouragement or counsel which at the parting hour they wish to speak to their loved ones.

Those who seek healing by prayer should not neglect to make use of the remedial agencies within their reach. It is not a denial of faith to use such remedies as God has provided to alleviate pain and to aid nature in her work of restoration. It is no denial of faith to co-operate with God, and to place themselves in the condition most favorable to recovery. God has put it in our power to obtain a knowledge of the laws of life. This knowledge has been placed within our reach for use.

We should employ every facility for the restoration of health, taking every advantage possible, working in harmony with natural laws. When we have prayed for the recovery of the sick, we can work with all the more energy, thanking God that we have the privilege of co-operating with Him, and asking His blessing on the means which He Himself has provided.

We have the sanction of the word of God for the use of remedial agencies. Hezekiah, king of Israel, was sick, and a prophet of God brought him the message that he should die. He cried unto the Lord, and the Lord heard His servant and sent him a message that fifteen years should be added to his life. Now, one word from God would have healed Hezekiah instantly; but special directions were given, "Let them take a lump of figs, and lay it for a plaster upon the boil, and he shall recover." Isaiah 38:21.

On one occasion Christ anointed the eyes of a blind man with clay and bade him, "Go, wash in the pool of Siloam. . . . He went his way therefore, and washed, and came seeing." John 9:7. The cure could be wrought only by the power of the Great Healer, yet Christ made use of the simple agencies of nature. While He did not give countenance to drug medication, He sanctioned the use of simple and natural remedies.

When we have prayed for the recovery of the sick, whatever the outcome of the case, let us not lose faith in God. If we are called upon to meet bereavement, let us accept the bitter cup, remembering that a Father's hand holds it to our lips. But should health be restored, it should not be forgotten that the recipient of healing mercy is placed under renewed obligation to the Creator. When the ten lepers were cleansed, only one returned to find Jesus and give Him glory. Let none of us be like the unthinking nine, whose hearts were untouched by the mercy of God. "Every good gift and every perfect gift is from above, and cometh down from the Father of lights, with whom is no variableness, neither shadow of turning." James 1:17.

NATURAL REMEDIES

Disease never comes without a cause. The way is prepared, and disease invited, by disregard of the laws of health. Many suffer in consequence of the transgression of their parents. While they are not responsible for what their parents have done, it is nevertheless their duty to ascertain what are and what are not violations of the laws of health. They should avoid the wrong habits of their parents and, by correct living, place themselves in better conditions.

The greater number, however, suffer because of their own wrong course of action. They disregard the principles of health by their habits of eating, drinking, dressing, and working. Their transgression of nature's laws produces the sure result; and when sickness comes upon them, many do not credit their suffering to the true cause, but murmur against God because of their afflictions. But God is not responsible for the suffering that follows disregard of natural law.

God has endowed us with a certain amount of vital force. He has also formed us with organs suited to maintain the various functions of life, and He designs that these organs shall work together in harmony. If we carefully preserve the life force, and keep the delicate mechanism of the body in order, the result is health; but if the vital force is too rapidly exhausted, the nervous system borrows power for present use from its resources of strength, and when one organ is injured, all are affected. Nature bears much abuse without apparent resistance; she then arouses and makes a determined effort to remove the effects of the ill-treatment she has suffered. Her effort to correct these conditions is often manifest in fever and various other forms of sickness.

When the abuse of health is carried so far that sickness results, the sufferer can often do for himself what no one else can do for him. The first thing to be done is to ascertain the true character of the sickness and then go to work intelligently to remove the cause. If the harmonious working of the system has become unbalanced by overwork, overeating, or other irregularities, do not endeavor to adjust the difficulties by adding a burden of poisonous medicines.

Intemperate eating is often the cause of sickness, and what nature most needs is to be relieved of the undue burden that has been placed upon her. In many cases of sickness, the very best remedy is for the patient to fast for a meal or two, that the overworked organs of digestion may have an opportunity to rest. A fruit diet for a few days has often brought great relief to brain workers. Many times a short period of entire abstinence from food, followed by simple, moderate eating, has led to recovery through nature's own recuperative effort. An abstemious diet for a month or two would convince many sufferers that the path of self-denial is the path to health.

Some make themselves sick by overwork. For these, rest, freedom from care, and a spare diet, are essential to restoration of health. To those who are brain weary and nervous because of continual labor and close confinement, a visit to the country, where they can live a simple, carefree life, coming in close contact with the things of nature, will be most helpful. Roaming through the fields and the woods, picking the flowers, listening to the songs of the birds, will do far more that any other agency toward their recovery.

In health and in sickness, pure water is one of heaven's choicest blessings. Its proper use promotes health. It is the beverage which God provided to quench the thirst of animals and man. Drunk freely, it helps to supply the necessities of the system and assists nature to resist disease. The external application of water is one of the easiest and most satisfactory ways of regulating the circulation of the blood. A cold or cool bath is an excellent tonic. Warm baths open the pores and thus aid in the elimination of impurities. Both warm and neutral baths soothe the nerves and equalize the circulation.

But many have never learned by experience the beneficial effects of the proper use of water, and they are afraid of it. Water treatments are not appreciated as they should be, and to apply them skillfully requires work that many are unwilling to perform. But none should feel excused for ignorance or indifference on this subject. There are many ways in which water can be applied to relieve pain and check disease. All should become intelligent in its use in simple home treatments. Mothers, especially, should know how to care for their families in both health and sickness.

Action is a law of our being. Every organ of the body has its appointed work, upon the performance of which its development and strength depend. The normal action of all the organs gives strength and vigor, while the tendency of disuse is toward decay and death.

Bind up an arm, even for a few weeks, then free it from its bands, and you will see that it is weaker than the one you have been using moderately during the same time. Inactivity produces the same effect upon the whole muscular system.

Inactivity is a fruitful cause of disease. Exercise quickens and equalizes the circulation of the blood, but in idleness the blood does not circulate freely, and the changes in it, so necessary to life and health, do not take place. The skin, too, becomes inactive. Impurities are not expelled as they would be if the circulation had been quickened by vigorous exercise, the skin kept in a healthy condition, and the lungs fed with plenty of pure, fresh air. This state of the system throws a double burden on the excretory organs, and disease is the result.

Invalids should not be encouraged in inactivity. When there has been serious overtaxation in any direction, entire rest for a time will sometimes ward off serious illness; but in the case of confirmed invalids, it is seldom necessary to suspend all activity.

Those who have broken down from mental labor should have rest from wearing thought; but they should not be led to believe that it is dangerous to use their mental powers at all. Many are inclined to regard their condition as worse than it really is. This state of mind is unfavorable to recovery, and should not be encouraged.

Ministers, teachers, students, and other brain workers often suffer from illness as the result of severe mental taxation, unrelieved by physical exercise. What these persons need is a more active life. Strictly temperate habits, combined with proper exercise, would ensure both mental and physical vigor, and would give power of endurance to all brain workers.

Those who have overtaxed their physical powers should not be encouraged to forgo manual labor entirely. But labor, to be of the greatest advantage, should be systematic and agreeable. Outdoor exercise is the best; it should be so planned as to strengthen by use the organs that have become weakened; and the heart should be in it; the labor of the hands should never degenerate into mere drudgery.

When invalids have nothing to occupy their time and attention, their thoughts become centered upon themselves, and they grow morbid and irritable. Many times they dwell upon their bad feelings until they think themselves much worse than they really are and wholly unable to do anything.

In all these cases well-directed physical exercise would prove an effective remedial agent. In some cases it is indispensable to the recovery of health. The will goes with the labor of the hands; and what these invalids need is to have the will aroused. When the will is dormant, the imagination becomes abnormal, and it is impossible to resist disease.

Inactivity is the greatest curse that could come upon most invalids. Light employment in useful labor, while it does not tax mind or body, has a happy influence upon both. It strengthens the muscles, improves the circulation, and gives the invalid the satisfaction of knowing that he is not wholly useless in this busy world. He may be able to do but little at first, but he will soon find his strength increasing, and the amount of work done can be increased accordingly.

Exercise aids the dyspeptic by giving the digestive organs a healthy tone. To engage in severe study or violent physical exercise immediately after eating, hinders the work of digestion; but a short walk after a meal, with the head erect and the shoulders back, is a great benefit.

Notwithstanding all that is said and written concerning its importance, there are still many who neglect physical exercise. Some grow corpulent because the system is clogged; others become thin and feeble because their vital powers are exhausted in disposing of an excess of food. The liver is burdened in its effort to cleanse the blood of impurities, and illness is the result.

Those whose habits are sedentary should, when the weather will permit, exercise in the open air every day, summer or winter. Walking is preferable to riding or driving, for it brings more of the muscles into exercise. The lungs are forced into healthy action, since it is impossible to walk briskly without inflating them.

Such exercise would in many cases be better for the health than medicine. Physicians often advise their patients to take an ocean voyage, to go to some mineral spring, or to visit different places for change of climate, when in most cases if they would eat temperately, and take cheerful, healthful exercise, they would recover health and would save time and money.

MIND CURE

The relation that exists between the mind and the body is very intimate. When one is affected, the other sympathizes. The condition of the mind affects the health to a far greater degree than many realize. Many of the diseases from which men suffer are the result of mental depression. Grief, anxiety, discontent, remorse, guilt, distrust, all tend to break down the life forces and to invite decay and death.

Disease is sometimes produced, and is often greatly aggravated, by the imagination. Many are lifelong invalids who might be well if they only thought so. Many imagine that every slight exposure will cause illness, and the evil effect is produced because it is expected. Many die from disease the cause of which is wholly imaginary.

Courage, hope, faith, sympathy, love, promote health and prolong life. A contented mind, a cheerful spirit, is health to the body and strength to the soul. "A merry [rejoicing] heart doeth good like a medicine." Proverbs 17:22.

In the treatment of the sick the effect of mental influence should not be overlooked. Rightly used, this influence affords one of the most effective agencies for combating disease.

CONTROL OF MIND OVER MIND - HYPNOTISM

There is, however, a form of mind cure that is one of the most effective agencies for evil. Through this so-called science, one mind is brought under the control of another so that the individuality of the weaker is merged in that of the stronger mind. One person acts out the will of another. Thus it is claimed that the tenor of the thoughts may be changed, that health-giving impulses may be imparted, and patients may be enabled to resist and overcome disease.

This method of cure has been employed by persons who were ignorant of its real nature and tendency, and who believed it to be a means of benefit to the sick. But the so-called science is based upon false principles. It is foreign to the nature and spirit of Christ. It does not lead to Him who is life and salvation. The one who attracts minds to himself leads them to separate from the true Source of their strength.

It is not God's purpose that any human being should yield his mind and will to the control of another, becoming a passive instrument in his hands. No one is to merge his individuality in that of another. He is not to look to any human being as the source of healing. His dependence must be in God. In the dignity of his God-given manhood he is to be controlled by God Himself, not by any human intelligence.

God desires to bring men into direct relation with Himself. In all His dealings with human beings He recognizes the principle of personal responsibility. He seeks to encourage a sense of personal dependence and to impress the need of personal guidance. He desires to bring the human into association with the divine, that men may be transformed into the divine likeness. Satan works to thwart this purpose. He seeks to encourage dependence upon men. When minds are turned away from God, the tempter can bring them under his rule. He can control humanity.

The theory of mind controlling mind was originated by Satan, to introduce himself as the chief worker, to put human philosophy where divine philosophy should be. Of all the errors that are finding acceptance among professedly Christian people, none is a more dangerous deception, none more certain to separate man from God, than is this. Innocent though it may appear, if exercised upon patients it will tend to their destruction, not to their restoration. It opens a door through which Satan will enter to take possession both of the mind that is given up to be controlled by another, and of the mind that controls.

Fearful is the power thus given to evil-minded men and women. What opportunities it affords to those who live by taking advantage of other's weaknesses or follies! How many, through control of minds feeble or diseased, will find a means of gratifying lustful passion or greed of gain!

There is something better for us to engage in than the control of humanity by humanity. The physician should educate the people to look from the human to the divine. Instead of teaching the sick to depend upon human beings for the cure of soul and body, he should direct them to the One who can save to the uttermost all who come unto Him. He who made man's mind knows what the mind needs.

God alone is the One who can heal. Those whose minds and bodies are diseased are to behold in Christ the restorer. "Because I live, He says, "ye shall live also." John 14:19. This is the life we are to present to the sick, telling them that if they have faith in Christ as the restorer, if they co-operate with Him, obeying the laws of health, and striving to perfect holiness in His fear, He will impart to them His life. When we present Christ to them in this way, we are imparting a power, a strength, that is of value; for it comes from above. This is the true science of healing for body and soul.

SYMPATHY

Great wisdom is needed in dealing with diseases caused through the mind. A sore, sick heart, a discouraged mind, needs mild treatment. Many times some living home trouble is, like a canker, eating to the very soul and weakening the life force. And sometimes it is the case that remorse for sin undermines the constitution and unbalances the mind. It is through tender sympathy that this class of invalids can be benefited. The physician should first gain their confidence and then point them to the Great Healer. If their faith can be directed to the True Physician, and they can have confidence that He has undertaken their case, this will bring relief to the mind and often give health to the body.

Sympathy and tact will often prove a greater benefit to the sick than will the most skillful treatment given in a cold, indifferent way. When a physician comes to the sickbed with a listless, careless manner, looks at the afflicted one with little concern, by word or action giving the impression that the case is not one requiring much attention, and then leaves the patient to his own reflections, he has done that patient positive harm. The doubt and discouragement produced by his indifference will often counteract the good effect of the remedies he may prescribe.

If physicians could put themselves in the place of the one whose spirit is humbled and whose will is weakened by suffering, and who longs for words of sympathy and assurance, they would be better prepared to appreciate his feelings. When the love and sympathy that Christ manifested for the sick is combined with the physician's knowledge, his very presence will be a blessing.

Frankness in dealing with a patient inspires him with confidence, and thus proves an important aid to recovery. There are physicians who consider it wise policy to conceal from the patient the nature and cause of the disease from which he is suffering. Many, fearing to excite or discourage a patient by stating the truth, will hold out false hopes of recovery, and even allow a patient to go down to the grave without warning him of his danger. All this is unwise. It may not always be safe or best to explain to the patient the full extent of his danger. This might alarm him and retard or even prevent recovery. Nor can the whole truth always be told to those whose ailments are largely imaginary. Many of these persons are unreasonable, and have not accustomed themselves to exercise self-control. They have peculiar fancies, and imagine many things that are false in regard to themselves and to others. To them these things are real, and those who care for them need to manifest constant kindness and unwearied patience and tact. If these patients were told the truth in regard to themselves, some would be offended, others discouraged. Christ said to His disciples, "I have yet many things to say unto you, but ye cannot bear them now." John 16:12. But though the truth may not all be spoken on all occasions, it is never necessary or justifiable to deceive. Never should the physician or the nurse stoop to prevarication. He who does this places himself where God cannot co-operate with him, and in forfeiting the confidence of his patients he is casting away one of the most effective human aids to their restoration.

The power of the will is not valued as it should be. Let the will be kept awake and rightly directed, and it will impart energy to the whole being and will be a wonderful aid in the maintenance of health. It is a power also in dealing with disease. Exercised in the right direction, it would control the imagination and be a potent means of resisting and overcoming disease of both mind and body. By the exercise of the will power in placing themselves in right relation to life, patients can do much to co-operate with the physician's efforts for their recovery. There are thousands who can recover health if they will. The Lord does not want them to be sick. He desires them to be well and happy, and they should make up their minds to be well. Often invalids can resist disease simply by refusing to yield to ailments and settle down in a state of inactivity. Rising above their aches and pains, let them engage in useful employment suited to their strength. By such employment and the free use of air and sunlight, many an emaciated invalid might recover health and strength.

BIBLE PRINCIPLES OF CURE

For those who would regain or preserve health there is a lesson in the words of Scripture, "Be not drunk with wine, wherein is excess; but be filled with the Spirit." Ephesians 5:18. Not through the excitement or oblivion produced by unnatural or unhealthful stimulants; not through indulgence of the lower appetites or passions, is to be found true healing or refreshment for the body or the soul. Among the sick are many who are without God and without hope. They suffer from ungratified desires, disordered passions, and the condemnation of their own consciences; they are losing their hold upon this life, and they have no prospect for the life to come. Let not the attendants upon the sick hope to benefit these patients by granting them frivolous, exciting indulgences. These have been the curse of their lives. The hungry, thirsting soul will continue to hunger and thirst so long as it seeks to find satisfaction here. Those who drink at the fountain of selfish pleasure are deceived. They mistake hilarity for strength, and when the excitement ceases, their inspiration ends, and they are left to discontent and despondency.

Abiding peace, true rest of spirit, has but one Source. It was of this that Christ spoke when He said, "Come unto Me, all ye that labor and are heavy-laden, and I will give you rest." Matthew 11:28. "Peace I leave with you, My peace I give unto you: not as the world giveth, give I unto you." John 14:27. This peace is not something that He gives apart from Himself. It is in Christ, and we can receive it only by receiving Him.

Christ is the wellspring of life. That which many need is to have a clearer knowledge of Him; they need to be patiently and kindly, yet earnestly, taught how the whole being may be thrown open to the healing agencies of heaven. When the sunlight of God's love illuminates the darkened chambers of the soul, restless weariness and dissatisfaction will cease, and satisfying joys will give vigor to the mind and health and energy to the body.

We are in a world of suffering. Difficulty, trial, and sorrow await us all along the way to the heavenly home. But there are many who make life's burdens doubly heavy by continually anticipating trouble. If they meet with adversity or disappointment they think that everything is going to ruin, that theirs is the hardest lot of all, that they are surely coming to want. Thus they bring wretchedness upon themselves and cast a shadow upon all around them. Life itself becomes a burden to them. But it need not be thus. It will cost a determined effort to change the current of their thought. But the change can be made. Their happiness, both for this life and for the life to come, depends upon their fixing their minds upon cheerful things. Let them look away from the dark picture, which is imaginary, to the benefits which God has strewn in their pathway, and beyond these to the unseen and eternal.

For every trial, God has provided help. When Israel in the desert came to the bitter waters of Marah, Moses cried unto the Lord. The Lord did not provide some new remedy; He called attention to that which was at hand. A shrub which He had created was to be cast into the fountain to make the water pure and sweet. When this was done, the people drank of the water and were refreshed. In every trial, if we seek Him, Christ will give us help. Our eyes will be opened to discern the healing promises recorded in His word. The Holy Spirit will teach us how to appropriate every blessing that will be an antidote to grief. For every bitter draft that is placed to our lips, we shall find a branch of healing.

We are not to let the future, with its hard problems, its unsatisfying prospects, make our hearts faint, our knees tremble, our hands hang down. "Let him take hold of My strength," says the Mighty One, "that he may make peace with Me; and he shall make peace with Me." Isaiah 27:5. Those who surrender their lives to His guidance and to His service will never be placed in a position for which He has not made provision. Whatever our situation, if we are doers of His word, we have a Guide to direct our way; whatever our perplexity, we have a sure Counselor; whatever our sorrow, bereavement, or loneliness, we have a sympathizing Friend.

If in our ignorance we make missteps, the Saviour does not forsake us. We need never feel that we are alone. Angels are our companions. The Comforter that Christ promised to send in His name abides with us. In the way that leads to the City of God there are no difficulties which those who trust in Him may not overcome. There are no dangers which they may not escape. There is not a sorrow, not a grievance, not a human weakness, for which He has not provided a remedy.

None need abandon themselves to discouragement and despair. Satan may come to you with the cruel suggestion, "Yours is a hopeless case. You are irredeemable." But there is hope for you in Christ. God does not bid us overcome in our own strength. He asks us to come close to His side. Whatever difficulties we labor under, which weigh down soul and body, He waits to make us free.

He who took humanity upon Himself knows how to sympathize with the sufferings of humanity. Not only does Christ know every soul, and the peculiar needs and trials of that soul, but He knows all the circumstances that chafe and perplex the spirit. His hand is outstretched in pitying tenderness to every suffering child. Those who suffer most have most of His sympathy and pity. He is touched with the feeling of our infirmities, and He desires us to lay our perplexities and troubles at His feet and leave them there.

It is not wise to look to ourselves and study our emotions. If we do this, the enemy will present difficulties and temptations that weaken faith and destroy courage. Closely to study our emotions and give way to our feelings is to entertain doubt and entangle ourselves in perplexity. We are to look away from self to Jesus.

When temptations assail you, when care, perplexity, and darkness seem to surround your soul, look to the place where you last saw the light. Rest in Christ's love and under His protecting care. When sin struggles for the mastery in the heart, when guilt oppresses the soul and burdens the conscience, when unbelief clouds the mind, remember that Christ's grace is sufficient to subdue sin and banish the darkness. Entering into communion with the Saviour, we enter the region of peace.

Nothing tends more to promote health of body and of soul than does a spirit of gratitude and praise. It is a positive duty to resist melancholy, discontented thoughts and feelings–as much a duty as it is to pray. If we are heaven-bound, how can we go as a band of mourners, groaning and complaining all along the way to our Father's house?

Those professed Christians who are constantly complaining, and who seem to think cheerfulness and happiness a sin, have not genuine religion. Those who take a mournful pleasure in all that is melancholy in the natural world, who choose to look upon dead leaves rather than to gather the beautiful living flowers, who see no beauty in grand mountain heights and in valleys clothed with living green, who close their senses to the joyful voice which speaks to them in nature, and which is sweet and musical to the listening ear–these are not in Christ. They are gathering to themselves gloom and darkness, when they might have brightness, even the Sun of Righteousness arising in their hearts with healing in His beams.

Often your mind may be clouded because of pain. Then do not try to think. You know that Jesus loves you. He understands your weakness. You may do His will by simply resting in His arms.

It is a law of nature that our thoughts and feelings are encouraged and strengthened as we give them utterance. While words express thoughts, it is also true that thoughts follow words. If we would give more expression to our faith, rejoice more in the blessings that we know we have,–the great mercy and love of God,–we should have more faith and greater joy. No tongue can express, no finite mind can conceive, the blessing that results from appreciating the goodness and love of God. Even on earth we may have joy as a wellspring, never failing, because fed by the streams that flow from the throne of God.

Then let us educate our hearts and lips to speak the praise of God for His matchless love. Let us educate our souls to be hopeful and to abide in the light shining from the cross of Calvary. Never should we forget that we are children of the heavenly King, sons and daughters of the Lord of hosts. It is our privilege to maintain a calm repose in God.

"Let the peace of God rule in your hearts; . . . and be ye thankful." Colossians 3:15. Forgetting our own difficulties and troubles, let us praise God for an opportunity to live for the glory of His name. Let the fresh blessings of each new day awaken praise in our hearts for these tokens of His loving care. When you open your eyes in the morning, thank God that He has kept you through the night. Thank Him for His peace in your heart. Morning, noon, and night, let gratitude as a sweet perfume ascend to heaven.

When someone asks how you are feeling, do not try to think of something mournful to tell in order to gain sympathy. Do not talk of your lack of faith and your sorrows and sufferings. The tempter delights to hear such words. When talking on gloomy subjects, you are glorifying him. We are not to dwell on the great power of Satan to overcome us. Often we give ourselves into his hands by talking of his power. Let us talk instead of the great power of God to bind up all our interests with His own. Tell of the matchless power of Christ, and speak of His glory. All heaven is interested in our salvation. The angels of God, thousands upon thousands, and ten thousand times ten thousand, are commissioned to minister to those who shall be heirs of salvation. They guard us against evil and press back the powers of darkness that are seeking our destruction. Have we not reason to be thankful every moment, thankful even when there are apparent difficulties in our pathway?

SING PRAISES

Let praise and thanksgiving be expressed in song. When tempted, instead of giving utterance to our feelings, let us by faith lift up a song of thanksgiving to God.

Song is a weapon that we can always use against discouragement. As we thus open the heart to the sunlight of the Saviour's presence, we shall have health and His blessing.

See Psalms 107:1,2; 105:2,3; 107:9-15; 42:11.

"In everything give thanks: for this is the will of God in Christ Jesus concerning you." I Thessalonians 5:18. This command is an assurance that even the things which appear to be against us will work for our good. God would not bid us be thankful for that which would do us harm. See Psalms 27:1; 27:5,6,R.V.; 40:1-3; 28:7.

One of the surest hindrances to the recovery of the sick is the centering of attention upon themselves. Many invalids feel that everyone should give them sympathy and help, when what they need is to have their attention turned away from themselves, to think of and care for others.

Often prayer is solicited for the afflicted, the sorrowful, the discouraged; and this is right. We should pray that God will shed light into the darkened mind and comfort the sorrowful heart. But God answers prayer for those who place themselves in the channel of His blessings. While we offer prayer for these sorrowful ones, we should encourage them to try to help those more needy than themselves. The darkness will be dispelled from their own hearts as they try to help others. As we seek to comfort others with the comfort wherewith we are comforted, the blessing comes back to us.

The fifty-eight chapter of Isaiah is a prescription for maladies of the body and of the soul. If we desire health and the true joy of life we must put into practice the rules given in this scripture. Of the service acceptable to Him, and its blessings, the Lord says:

"Is it not to deal thy bread to the hungry,

And that thou bring the poor that are cast out to thy house? When thou seest the naked, that thou cover him;

And that thou hide not thyself from thine own flesh?

Then shall thy light break forth as the morning,

And thine health shall spring forth speedily: And thy righteousness shall go before thee; The glory of the Lord shall be thy rearward.

Then shalt thou call, and the Lord shall answer; Thou shalt cry, and He shall say, Here I am.

If thou take away from the midst of thee the yoke, The putting forth of the finger, and speaking vanity; And if thou draw out thy soul to the hungry,

And satisfy the afflicted soul;
Then shall thy light rise in obscurity,
And thy darkness be as the noonday:
And the Lord shall guide thee continually,
And satisfy thy soul in drought,
And make fat thy bones:
And thou shalt be like a watered garden,
And like a spring of water,
Whose waters fail not."
Isaiah 58:7-11.

Good deeds are twice a blessing, benefiting both the giver and the receiver of the kindness. The consciousness of right-doing is one of the best medicines for diseased bodies and minds. When the mind is free and happy from a sense of duty well done and the satisfaction of giving happiness to others, the cheering, uplifting influence brings new life to the whole being.

Let the invalid, instead of constantly requiring sympathy, seek to impart it. Let the burden of your own weakness and sorrow and pain be cast upon the compassionate Saviour. Open your heart to His love, and let it flow out to others. Remember that all have trials hard to bear, temptations hard to resist, and you may do something to lighten these burdens. Express gratitude for the blessings you have; show appreciation of the attentions you receive. Keep the heart full of the precious promises of God, that you may bring forth from this treasure, words that will be a comfort and strength to others. This will surround you with an atmosphere that will be helpful and uplifting. Let it be your aim to bless those around you, and you will find ways of being helpful, both to the members of your own family and to others.

If those who are suffering from ill-health would forget self in their interest for others; if they would fulfill the Lord's command to minister to those more needy than themselves, they would realize the truthfulness of the prophetic promise, "Then shall thy light break forth as the morning, and thine health shall spring forth speedily."

IN CONTACT WITH NATURE

The Creator chose for our first parents the surroundings best adapted for their health and happiness. He did not place them in a palace or surround them with the artificial adornments and luxuries that so many today are struggling to obtain. He placed them in close touch with nature and in close communion with the holy ones of heaven.

In the garden that God prepared as a home for His children, graceful shrubs and delicate flowers greeted the eye at every turn. There were trees of every variety, many of them laden with fragrant and delicious fruit. On their branches the birds caroled their songs of praise. Under their shadow the creatures of the earth sported together without a fear.

Adam and Eve, in their untainted purity, delighted in the sights and sounds of Eden. God appointed them their work in the garden, "to dress it and to keep it." Genesis 2:15. Each day's labor brought them health and gladness, and the happy pair greeted with joy the visits of their Creator, as in the cool of the day He walked and talked with them. Daily God taught them His lessons.

The plan of life which God appointed for our first parents has lessons for us. Although sin has cast its shadow over the earth, God desires His children to find delight in the works of His hands. The more closely His plan of life is followed, the more wonderfully will He work to restore suffering humanity. The sick need to be brought into close touch with nature. An outdoor life amid natural surroundings would work wonders for many a helpless and almost hopeless invalid.

The noise and excitement and confusion of the cities, their constrained and artificial life, are most wearisome and exhausting to the sick. The air, laden with smoke and dust, with poisonous gases, and with germs of disease, is a peril to life. The sick, for the most part shut within four walls, come almost to feel as if they were prisoners in their rooms. They look out on houses and pavements and hurrying crowds, with perhaps not even a glimpse of blue sky or sunshine, of grass or flower or tree. Shut up in this way, they brood over their suffering and sorrow, and become a prey to their own sad thoughts.

And for those who are weak in moral power, the cities abound in dangers. In them, patients who have unnatural appetites to overcome are continually exposed to temptation. They need to be placed amid new surroundings where the current of their thoughts will be changed; they need to be placed under influences wholly different from those that have wrecked their lives. Let them for a season be removed from those influences that lead away from God, into a purer atmosphere.

Institutions for the care of the sick would be far more successful if they could be established away from the cities. And so far as possible, all who are seeking to recover health should place themselves amid country surroundings where they can have the benefit of outdoor life. Nature is God's physician. The pure air, the glad sunshine, the flowers and trees, the orchards and vineyards, and outdoor exercise amid these surroundings, are health-giving, life-giving.

Physicians and nurses should encourage their patients to be much in the open air. Outdoor life is the only remedy that many invalids need. It has a wonderful power to heal diseases caused by the excitements and excesses of fashionable life, a life that weakens and destroys the powers of body, mind, and soul.

How grateful to the invalids weary of city life, the glare of many lights, and the noise of the streets, are the quiet and freedom of the country! How eagerly do they turn to the scenes of nature! How glad would they be to sit in the open air, rejoice in the sunshine, and breathe the fragrance of tree and flower! There are life-giving properties in the balsam of the pine, in the fragrance of the cedar and the fir, and other trees also have properties that are health restoring.

To the chronic invalid, nothing so tends to restore health and happiness as living amid attractive country surroundings. Here the most helpless ones can sit or lie in the sunshine or in the shade of the trees. They have only to lift their eyes to see above them the beautiful foliage. A sweet sense of restfulness and refreshing comes over them as they listen to the murmuring of the breezes. The drooping spirits revive. The waning strength is recruited. Unconsciously the mind becomes peaceful, the fevered pulse more calm and regular. As the sick grow stronger, they will venture to take a few steps to gather some of the lovely flowers, precious messengers of God's love to His afflicted family here below.

Plans should be devised for keeping patients out of doors. For those who are able to work, let some pleasant, easy employment be provided. Show them how agreeable and helpful this outdoor work is. Encourage them to breathe the fresh air. Teach them to breathe deeply, and in breathing and speaking to exercise the abdominal muscles. This is an education that will be invaluable to them.

Exercise in the open air should be prescribed as a life-giving necessity. And for such exercises there is nothing better than the cultivation of the soil. Let patients have flower beds to care for, or work to do in the orchard or vegetable garden. As they are encouraged to leave their rooms and spend time in the open air, cultivating flowers or doing some other light, pleasant work, their attention will be diverted from themselves and their sufferings.

The more the patient can be kept out of doors, the less care will he require. The more cheerful his surroundings, the more helpful will he be. Shut up in the house, be it ever so elegantly furnished, he will grow fretful and gloomy. Surround him with the beautiful things of nature; place him where he can see the flowers growing and hear the birds singing, and his heart will break into song in harmony with the songs of the birds. Relief will come to body and mind. The intellect will be awakened, the imagination quickened, and the mind prepared to appreciate the beauty of God's word.

In nature may always be found something to divert the attention of the sick from themselves and direct their thoughts to God. Surrounded by His wonderful works, their minds are uplifted from the things that are seen to the things that are unseen. The beauty of nature leads them to think of the heavenly home, where there will be nothing to mar the loveliness, nothing to taint or destroy, nothing to cause disease or death.

Let physicians and nurses draw from the things of nature, lessons teaching of God. Let them point the patients to Him whose hand has made the lofty trees, the grass, and the flowers, encouraging them to see in every bud and flower an expression of His love for His children. He who cares for the birds and the flowers will care for the beings formed in His own image.

Out of doors, amid the things that God has made, breathing the fresh, health-giving air, the sick can best be told of the new life in

Christ. Here God's word can be read. Here the light of Christ's righteousness can shine into hearts darkened by sin. O, could I find, from day to day, A nearness to my God, Then would my hours glide sweet away, While leaning on His word.

Men and women in need of physical and spiritual healing are to be thus brought into contact with those whose words and acts will draw them to Christ. They are to be brought under the influence of the great Medical Missionary, who can heal both soul and body. They are to hear the story of the Saviour's love, of the pardon freely provided for all who come to Him confessing their sins.

Under such influences as these, many suffering ones will be guided into the way of life. Angels of heaven co-operate with human instrumentalities in bringing encouragement and hope and joy and peace to the hearts of the sick and suffering. Under such conditions the sick are doubly blessed, and many find health. The feeble step recovers its elasticity. The eye regains its brightness. The hopeless become hopeful. The once despondent countenance wears an expression of joy. The complaining tones of the voice give place to tones of cheerfulness and content.

As physical health is regained, men and women are better able to exercise that faith in Christ which secures the health of the soul. In the consciousness of sins forgiven there is inexpressible peace and joy and rest. The clouded hope of the Christian is brightened. The words express the belief, "God is our refuge and strength, a very pleasant help in trouble." "Yea, though I walk through the valley of the shadow of death, I will fear no evil: for Thou art with me; Thy rod and Thy staff they comfort me." "He giveth power to the faint; and to them that have no might He increaseth strength." Psalms 46:1; 23:4; Isaiah 40:29.

HELPING THE TEMPTED

Not because we first loved Him did Christ love us; but "while we were yet sinners" He died for us. He does not treat us according to our desert. Although our sins have merited condemnation, He does not condemn us. Year after year He has borne with our weakness and ignorance, with our ingratitude and waywardness. Notwithstanding our wanderings, our hardness of heart, our neglect of His Holy Word, His hand is stretched out still.

Grace is an attribute of God exercised toward undeserving human beings. We did not seek for it, but it was sent in search of us. God rejoices to bestow His grace upon us, not because we are worthy, but because we are so utterly unworthy. Our only claim to His mercy is our great need.

The Lord God through Jesus Christ holds out His hand all the day long in invitation to the sinful and fallen. He will receive all. He welcomes all. It is His glory to pardon the chief of sinners. He will take the prey from the mighty, He will deliver the captive, He will pluck the brand from the burning. He will lower the golden chain of His mercy to the lowest depths of human wretchedness, and lift up the debased soul contaminated with sin.

Every human being is the object of loving interest to Him who gave His life that He might bring men back to God. Souls guilty and helpless, liable to be destroyed by the arts and snares of Satan, are cared for as a shepherd cares for the sheep of his flock.

The Saviour's example is to be the standard of our service for the tempted and the erring. The same interest and tenderness and long-suffering that He has manifested toward us, we are to manifest toward others. "As I have loved you," He says, "that ye also love one another." John 13:34. If Christ dwells in us, we shall reveal His unselfish love toward all with whom we have to do. As we see men and women in need of sympathy and help, we shall not ask, "Are they worthy?" but "How can I benefit them?"

Rich and poor, high and low, free and bond, are God's heritage. He who gave His life to redeem man sees in every human being a value that exceeds finite computation. By the mystery and glory of the cross we are to discern His estimate of the value of the soul. When we do this, we shall feel that human beings, however degraded, have cost too much to be treated with coldness or contempt. We shall realize the importance of working for our fellow men, that they may be exalted to the throne of God.

The lost coin, in the Saviour's parable, though lying in the dirt and rubbish, was a piece of silver still. Its owner sought it because it was of value. So every soul, however degraded by sin, is in God's sight accounted precious. As the coin bore the image and superscription of the reigning power, so man at his creation bore the image and superscription of God. Though now marred and dim through the influence of sin, the traces of this inscription remain upon every soul. God desires to recover that soul and to retrace upon it His own image in righteousness and holiness.

How little do we enter into sympathy with Christ on that which should be the strongest bond of union between us and Him—compassion for depraved, guilty, suffering souls, dead in trespasses and sins! The inhumanity of man toward man is our greatest sin. Many think that they are representing the justice of God while they wholly fail of representing His tenderness and His great love. Often the ones whom they meet with sternness and severity are under the stress of temptation. Satan is wrestling with these souls, and harsh, unsympathetic words discourage them and cause them to fall a prey to the tempter's power.

It is a delicate matter to deal with minds. Only He who reads the heart knows how to bring men to repentance. Only His wisdom can give us success in reaching the lost. You may stand up stiffly, feeling, "I am holier than thou," and it matters not how correct your reasoning or how true your words; they will never touch hearts. The love of Christ, manifested in word and act, will win its way to the soul, when the reiteration of precept or argument would accomplish nothing.

We need more of Christlike sympathy; not merely sympathy for those who appear to us to be faultless, but sympathy for poor, suffering, struggling souls, who are often overtaken in fault, sinning and repenting, tempted and discouraged. We are to go to our fellow men, touched, like our merciful High Priest, with the feeling of their infirmities.

It was the outcast, the publican and sinner, the despised of the nations, that Christ called and by His loving-kindness compelled to come unto Him. The one class that He would never countenance was those who stood apart in their self-esteem and looked down upon others.

"Go out into the highways and hedges, and compel them to come in," Christ bids us, "that My house may be filled." In obedience to this word we must go to the heathen who are near us, and to those who are afar off. The "publicans and harlots" must hear the Saviour's invitation. Through the kindness and long-suffering of His messengers the invitation becomes a compelling power to uplift those who are sunken in the lowest depths of sin.

Christian motives demand that we work with a steady purpose, an undying interest, an ever-increasing importunity, for the souls whom Satan is seeking to destroy. Nothing is to chill the earnest, yearning energy for the salvation of the lost. Mark how all through the word of God there is manifest the spirit of urgency, of imploring men and women to come to Christ. We must seize upon every opportunity, in private and in public, presenting every argument, urging every motive of infinite weight, to draw men to the Saviour. With all our power we must urge them to look unto Jesus and to accept His life of self-denial and sacrifice. We must show that we expect them to give joy to the heart of Christ by using every one of His gifts in honoring His name.

WORKING FOR THE INTEMPERATE

Every true reform has its place in the work of the gospel and tends to the uplifting of the soul to a new and nobler life. Especially does the temperance reform demand the support of Christian workers. They should call attention to this work and make it a living issue. Everywhere they should present to the people the principles of true temperance and call for signers to the temperance pledge. Earnest effort should be made in behalf of those who are in bondage to evil habits.

There is everywhere a work to be done for those who through intemperance have fallen. In the midst of churches, religious institutions, and professedly Christian homes, many of the youth are choosing the path to destruction. Through intemperate habits they bring upon themselves disease, and through greed to obtain money for sinful indulgence they fall into dishonest practices. Health and character are ruined. Aliens from God, outcasts from society, these poor souls feel that they are without hope either for this life or for the life to come. The hearts of the parents are broken. Men speak of these erring ones as hopeless; but not so does God regard them. He understands all the circumstances that have made them what they are, and He looks upon them with pity. This is a class that demand help. Never give them occasion to say, "No man cares for my soul."

Among the victims of intemperance are men of all classes and all professions. Men of high station, of eminent talents, of great attainments, have yielded to the indulgence of appetite until they are helpless to resist temptation. Some of them who were once in the possession of wealth are without home, without friends, in suffering, misery, disease, and degradation. They have lost their self-control. Unless a helping hand is held out to them, they will sink lower and lower. With these self-indulgence is not only a moral sin, but a physical disease.

Often in helping the intemperate we must, as Christ so often did, give first attention to their physical condition. They need wholesome, unstimulating food and drink, clean clothing, opportunity to secure physical cleanliness. They need to be surrounded with an atmosphere of helpful, uplifting Christian influence. In every city a place should be provided where the slaves of evil habit may receive help to break the chains that bind them. Strong drink is regarded by many as the only solace in trouble; but this need not be, if, instead of acting the part of the priest and Levite, professed Christians would follow the example of the good Samaritan.

In dealing with the victims of intemperance we must remember that we are not dealing with sane men, but with those who for the time being are under the power of a demon. Be patient and forbearing. Think not of the repulsive, forbidding appearance, but of the precious life that Christ died to redeem. As the drunkard awakens to a sense of his degradation, do all in your power to show that you are his friend. Speak no word of censure. Let no act or look express reproach or aversion. Very likely the poor soul curses himself. Help him to rise. Speak words that will encourage faith. Seek to strengthen every good trait in his character. Teach him how to reach upward. Show him that it is possible for him to live so as to win the respect of his fellow men. Help him to see the value of the talents which God has given him, but which he has neglected to improve.

Although the will has been depraved and weakened, there is hope for him in Christ. He will awaken in the heart higher impulses and holier desires. Encourage him to lay hold of the hope set before him in the gospel. Open the Bible before the tempted, struggling one, and over and over again read to him the promises of God. These promises will be to him as the leaves of the tree of life. Patiently continue your efforts, until with grateful joy the trembling hand grasps the hope of redemption through Christ.

You must hold fast to those whom you are trying to help, else victory will never be yours. They will be continually tempted to evil. Again and again they will be almost overcome by the craving for strong drink; again and again they may fall; but do not, because of this, cease your efforts.

They have decided to make an effort to live for Christ; but their will power is weakened, and they must be carefully guarded by those who watch for souls as they that must give an account. They have lost their manhood, and this they must win back. Many have to battle against strong hereditary tendencies to evil. Unnatural cravings, sensual impulses, were their inheritance from birth. These must be carefully guarded against. Within and without, good and evil are striving for the mastery. Those who have never passed through such experiences cannot know the almost overmastering power of appetite or the fierceness of the conflict between habits of self-indulgence and the determination to be temperate in all things. Over and over again the battle must be fought.

Many who are drawn to Christ will not have moral courage to continue the warfare against appetite and passion. But the worker must not be discouraged by this. Is it only those rescued from the lowest depths that backslide?

Remember that you do not work alone. Ministering angels unite in service with every truehearted son and daughter of God. And Christ is the restorer. The Great Physician Himself stands beside His faithful workers, saying to the repentant soul, "Child, thy sins be forgiven thee." Mark 2:5, A.R.V. margin.

Many are the outcasts who will grasp the hope set before them in the gospel and will enter the kingdom of heaven, while others who were blessed with great opportunities and great light which they did not improve will be left in outer darkness.

The victims of evil habit must be aroused to the necessity of making an effort for themselves. Others may put forth the most earnest endeavor to uplift them, the grace of God may be freely offered, Christ may entreat, His angels may minister; but all will be in vain unless they themselves are roused to fight the battle in their own behalf.

The last words of David to Solomon, then a young man, and soon to receive the crown of Israel, were, "Be... strong,... and show thyself a man." 1 Kings 2:2. To every child of humanity, the candidate for an immortal crown, are these words of inspiration spoken, "Be... strong, ... and show thyself a man."

The self-indulgent must be led to see and feel that great moral renovation is necessary if they would be men. God calls upon them to arouse and in the strength of Christ win back the God-given manhood that has been sacrificed through sinful indulgence.

Feeling the terrible power of temptation, the drawing of desire that leads to indulgence, many a man cries in despair, "I cannot resist evil." Tell him that he can, that he must resist. He may have been overcome again and again, but it need not be always thus. He is weak in moral power, controlled by the habits of a life of sin. His promises and resolutions are like ropes of sand. The knowledge of his broken promises and forfeited pledges weakens his confidence in his own sincerity and causes him to feel that God cannot accept him or work with his efforts. But he need not despair.

Those who put their trust in Christ are not to be enslaved by any heredity or cultivated habit or tendency. Instead of being held in bondage to the lower nature, they are to rule every appetite and passion. God has not left us to battle with evil in our own finite strength. Whatever may be our inherited or cultivated tendencies to wrong, we can overcome through the power that He is ready to impart.

THE POWER OF THE WILL

The tempted one needs to understand the true force of the will. This is the governing power in the nature of man–the power of decision, of choice. Everything depends on the right action of the will. Desires for goodness and purity are right, so far as they go; but if we stop here, they avail nothing. Many will go down to ruin while hoping and desiring to overcome their evil propensities. They do not yield the will to God. They do not choose to serve Him.

God has given us the power of choice; it is ours to exercise. We cannot change our hearts, we cannot control our thoughts, our impulses, our affections. We cannot make ourselves pure, fit for God's service. But we can choose to serve God, we can give Him our will; then He will work in us to will and to do according to His good pleasure. Thus our whole nature will be brought under the control of Christ.

Through the right exercise of the will, an entire change may be made in the life. By yielding up the will to Christ, we ally ourselves with divine power. We receive strength from above to hold us steadfast. A pure and noble life, a life of victory over appetite and lust, is possible to everyone who will unite his weak, wavering human will to the omnipotent, unwavering will of God.

Those who are struggling against the power of appetite should be instructed in the principles of healthful living. They should be shown that violation of the laws of health, by creating diseased conditions and unnatural cravings, lays the foundation of the liquor habit. Only by living in obedience to the principles of health can they hope to be freed from the craving for unnatural stimulants. While they depend upon divine strength to break the bonds of appetite, they are to co-operate with God by obedience to His laws, both moral and physical.

Those who are endeavoring to reform should be provided with employment. None who are able to labor should be taught to expect food and clothing and shelter free of cost. For their own sake, as well as for the sake of others, some way should be devised whereby they may return an equivalent for what they receive. Encourage every effort toward self-support. This will strengthen self-respect and a noble independence. And occupation of mind and body in useful work is essential as a safeguard against temptation.

DISAPPOINTMENTS; DANGERS

Those who work for the fallen will be disappointed in many who give promise of reform. Many will make but a superficial change in their habits and practices. They are moved by impulse, and for a time may seem to have reformed; but there is no real change of heart. They cherish the same self-love, have the same hungering for foolish pleasures, the same desire for self-indulgence. They have not a knowledge of the work of character building, and they cannot be relied upon as men of principle. They have debased their mental and spiritual powers by the gratification of appetite and passion, and this makes them weak. They are fickle and changeable. Their impulses tend toward sensuality. These persons are often a source of danger to others. Being looked upon as reformed men and women, they are trusted with responsibilities and are placed where their influence corrupts the innocent.

Even those who are sincerely seeking to reform are not beyond the danger of falling. They need to be treated with great wisdom as well as tenderness. The disposition to flatter and exalt those who have been rescued from the lowest depths sometimes proves their ruin. The practice of inviting men and women to relate in public the experience of their life of sin is full of danger to both speaker and hearers. To dwell upon scenes of evil is corrupting to mind and soul. And the prominence given to the rescued ones is harmful to them. Many are led to feel that their sinful life has given them a certain distinction. A love of notoriety and a spirit of self-trust are encouraged that prove fatal to the soul. Only in distrust of self and dependence on the mercy of Christ can they stand.

All who give evidence of true conversion should be encouraged to work for others. Let none turn away a soul who leaves the service of Satan for the service of Christ. When one gives evidence that the Spirit of God is striving with him, present every encouragement for entering the Lord's service. "Of some have compassion, making a difference." Jude 22. Those who are wise in the wisdom that comes from God will see souls in need of help, those who have sincerely repented, but who without encouragement would hardly dare to lay hold of hope. The Lord will put it into the hearts of His servants to welcome these trembling, repentant ones to their loving fellowship. Whatever may have been their besetting sins, however low they may have fallen, when in contrition they come to Christ, He receives them. Then give them something to do for Him. If they desire to labor in uplifting others from the pit of destruction from which they themselves were rescued, give them opportunity. Bring them into association with experienced Christians, that they may gain spiritual strength. Fill their hearts and hands with work for the Master.

When light flashes into the soul, some who appeared to be most fully given to sin will become successful workers for just such sinners as they themselves once were. Through faith in Christ some will rise to high places of service and be entrusted with responsibilities in the work of saving souls. They see where their own weakness lies, they realize the depravity of their nature. They know the strength of sin, the power of evil habit. They realize their inability to overcome without the help of Christ, and their constant cry is, "I cast my helpless soul on Thee."

These can help others. The one who has been tempted and tried, whose hope was well-nigh gone, but who was saved by hearing a message of love, can understand the science of soulsaving. He whose heart is filled with love for Christ because he himself has been sought for by the Saviour and brought back to the fold, knows how to seek the lost.

He can point sinners to the Lamb of God. He has given himself without reserve to God and has been accepted in the Beloved. The hand that in weakness was held out for help has been grasped. By the ministry of such ones many prodigals will be brought to the Father.

For every soul struggling to rise from a life of sin to a life of purity, the great element of power abides in the only "name under heaven given among men, whereby we must be saved." Acts 4:12. "If any man thirst" for restful hope, for deliverance from sinful propensities, Christ says, "let him come unto Me, and drink." John 7:37. The only remedy for vice is the grace and power of Christ.

The good resolutions made in one's own strength avail nothing. Not all the pledges in the world will break the power of evil habit. Never will men practice temperance in all things until their hearts are renewed by divine grace. We cannot keep ourselves from sin for one moment. Every moment we are dependent upon God.

True reformation begins with soul cleansing. Our work for the fallen will achieve real success only as the grace of Christ reshapes the character and the soul is brought into living connection with God.

Christ lived a life of perfect obedience to God's law, and in this He set an example for every human being. The life that He lived in this world we are to live through His power and under His instruction.

In our work for the fallen the claims of the law of God and the need of loyalty to Him are to be impressed on mind and heart. Never fail to show that there is a marked difference between the one who serves God and the one who serves Him not. God is love, but He cannot excuse willful disregard for His commands. The enactments of His government are such that men do not escape the consequences of disloyalty. Only those who honor Him can He honor. Man's conduct in this world decides his eternal destiny. As he has sown, so he must reap. Cause will be followed by effect.

Nothing less than perfect obedience can meet the standard of God's requirement. He has not left His requirements indefinite. He has enjoined nothing that is not necessary in order to bring man into harmony with Him. We are to point sinners to His ideal of character and to lead them to Christ, by whose grace only can this ideal be reached.

The Saviour took upon Himself the infirmities of humanity and lived a sinless life, that men might have no fear that because of the weakness of human nature they could not overcome. Christ came to make us "partakers of the divine nature," and His life declares that humanity, combined with divinity, does not commit sin.

The Saviour overcame to show man how he may overcome. All the temptations of Satan, Christ met with the word of God. By trusting in God's promises, He received power to obey God's commandments, and the tempter could gain no advantage. To every temptation His answer was, "It is written." So God has given us His word wherewith to resist evil. Exceeding great and precious promises are ours, that by these we "might be partakers of the divine nature, having escaped the corruption that is in the world through lust." 2 Peter 1:4.

Bid the tempted one look not to circumstances, to the weakness of self, or to the power of temptation, but to the power of God's word. All its strength is ours. "Thy word," says the psalmist, "have I hid in mine heart, that I might not sin against Thee." "By the word of Thy lips I have kept me from the paths of the destroyer." Psalms 119:11; 17:4.

Talk courage to the people; lift them up to God in prayer. Many who have been overcome by temptation are humiliated by their failures, and they feel that it is in vain for them to approach unto God; but this thought is of the enemy's suggestion. When they have sinned, and feel that they cannot pray, tell them that it is then the time to pray. Ashamed they may be, and deeply humbled; but as they confess their sins, He who is faithful and just will forgive their sins and cleanse them from all unrighteousness.

Nothing is apparently more helpless, yet really more invincible, than the soul that feels its nothingness and relies wholly on the merits of the Saviour. By prayer, by the study of His word, by faith in His abiding presence, the weakest of human beings may live in contact with the living Christ, and He will hold them by a hand that will never let go.

Those whom Christ has forgiven most will love Him most. These are they who in the final day will stand nearest to His throne.

"They shall see His face; and His name shall be in their foreheads." Revelation 22:4

FLESH AS FOOD

The diet appointed man in the beginning did not include animal food. Not till after the Flood, when every green thing on the earth had been destroyed, did man receive permission to eat flesh.

In choosing man's food in Eden, the Lord showed what was the best diet; in the choice made for Israel He taught the same lesson. He brought the Israelites out of Egypt and undertook their training, that they might be a people for His own possession. Through them He desired to bless and teach the world. He provided them with the food best adapted for this purpose, not flesh, but manna, "the bread of heaven." It was only because of their discontent and their murmuring for the fleshpots of Egypt that animal food was granted them, and this only for a short time. Its use brought disease and death to thousands. Yet the restriction to a nonflesh diet was never heartily accepted. It continued to be the cause of discontent and murmuring, open or secret, and it was not made permanent.

Upon their settlement in Canaan, the Israelites were permitted the use of animal food, but under careful restrictions which tended to lessen the evil results. The use of swine's flesh was prohibited, as also of other animals and of birds and fish whose flesh was pronounced unclean. Of the meats permitted, the eating of the fat and the blood was strictly forbidden.

Only such animals could be used for food as were in good condition. No creature that was torn, that had died of itself, or from which the blood had not been carefully drained, could be used as food.

By departing from the plan divinely appointed for their diet, the Israelites suffered great loss. They desired a flesh diet, and they reaped its results. They did not reach God's ideal of character or fulfill His purpose. The Lord "gave them their request; but sent leanness into their soul." Psalm 106:15. They valued the earthly above the spiritual, and the sacred pre-eminence which was His purpose for them they did not attain.

REASONS FOR DISCARDING FLESH FOODS

Those who eat flesh are but eating grains and vegetables at

second hand; for the animal receives from these things the nutrition that produces growth. The life that was in the grains and vegetables passes into the eater. We receive it by eating the flesh of the animal. How much better to get it direct, by eating the food that God provided for our use!

Flesh was never the best food; but its use is now doubly objectionable, since disease in animals is so rapidly increasing. Those who use flesh foods little know what they are eating. Often if they could see the animals when living and know the quality of the meat they eat, they would turn from it with loathing. People are continually eating flesh that is filled with tuberculous and cancerous germs. Tuberculosis, cancer, and other fatal diseases are thus communicated.

The tissues of the swine swarm with parasites. Of the swine God said, "It is unclean unto you: ye shall not eat of their flesh, nor touch their dead carcass." Deuteronomy 14:8. This command was given because swine's flesh is unfit for food. Swine are scavengers, and this is the only use they were intended to serve. Never, under any circumstances, was their flesh to be eaten by human beings. It is impossible for the flesh of any living creature to be wholesome when filth is its natural element and when it feeds upon every detestable thing.

Often animals are taken to market and sold for food when they are so diseased that their owners fear to keep them longer. And some of the processes of fattening them for market produce disease. Shut away from the light and pure air, breathing the atmosphere of filthy stables, perhaps fattening on decaying food, the entire body soon becomes contaminated with foul matter.

Animals are often transported long distances and subjected to great suffering in reaching a market. Taken from the green pastures, and traveling for weary miles over the hot, dusty roads, or crowded into filthy cars, feverish and exhausted, often for many hours deprived of food and water, the poor creatures are driven to their death, that human beings may feast on the carcasses.

In many places fish become so contaminated by the filth on which they feed as to be a cause of disease. This is especially the case where the fish come in contact with the sewage of large cities. The fish that are fed on the contents of the drains may pass into distant waters and may be caught where the water is pure and fresh. Thus when used as food they bring disease and death on those who do not suspect the danger.

The effects of a flesh diet may not be immediately realized; but this is no evidence that it is not harmful. Few can be made to believe that it is the meat they have eaten which has poisoned their blood and caused their suffering. Many die of diseases wholly due to meat eating, while the real cause is not suspected by themselves or by others.

The moral evils of a flesh diet are not less marked than are the physical ills. Flesh food is injurious to health, and whatever affects the body has a corresponding effect on the mind and the soul. Think of the cruelty to animals that meat eating involves, and its effect on those who inflict and those who behold it. How it destroys the tenderness with which we should regard these creatures of God!

The intelligence displayed by many dumb animals approaches so closely to human intelligence that it is a mystery. The animals see and hear and love and fear and suffer. They use their organs far more faithfully than many human beings use theirs. They manifest sympathy and tenderness toward their companions in suffering. Many animals show an affection for those who have charge of them, far superior to the affection shown by some of the human race. They form attachments for man which are not broken without great suffering to them.

What man with a human heart, who has ever cared for domestic animals, could look into their eyes, so full of confidence and affection, and willingly give them over to the butcher's knife? How could he devour their flesh as a sweet morsel?

It is a mistake to suppose that muscular strength depends on the use of animal food. The needs of the system can be better supplied, and more vigorous health can be enjoyed, without its use. The grains, with fruits, nuts, and vegetables, contain all the nutritive properties necessary to make good blood. These elements are not so well or so fully supplied by a flesh diet. Had the use of flesh been essential to health and strength, animal food would have been included in the diet appointed man in the beginning.

When the use of flesh food is discontinued, there is often a sense of weakness, a lack of vigor. Many urge this as evidence that flesh food is essential; but it is because foods of this class are stimulating, because they fever the blood and excite the nerves, that they are so missed. Some will find it as difficult to leave off flesh eating as it is for the drunkard to give up his dram; but they will be the better for the change.

When flesh food is discarded, its place should be supplied with a variety of grains, nuts, vegetables, and fruits that will be both nourishing and appetizing. This is especially necessary in the case of those who are weak or who are taxed with continuous labor. In some countries where poverty abounds, flesh is the cheapest food. Under these circumstances the change will be made with greater difficulty; but it can be effected. We should, however, consider the situation of the people and the power of lifelong habit, and should be careful not to urge even right ideas unduly. None should be urged to make the change abruptly. The place of meat should be supplied with wholesome foods that are inexpensive. In this matter very much depends on the cook. With care and skill, dishes may be prepared that will be both nutritious and appetizing, and will, to a great degree, take the place of flesh food.

In all cases educate the conscience, enlist the will, supply good, wholesome food, and the change will be readily made, and the demand for flesh will soon cease.

Is it not time that all should aim to dispense with flesh foods? How can those who are seeking to become pure, refined, and holy, that they may have the companionship of heavenly angels, continue to use as food anything that has so harmful an effect on soul and body? How can they take the life of God's creatures that they may consume the flesh as a luxury? Let them, rather, return to the wholesome and delicious food given to man in the beginning, and themselves practice, and teach their children to practice, mercy toward the dumb creatures that God has made and has placed under our dominion.

EXTREMES IN DIET

Not all who profess to believe in dietetic reform are really reformers. With many persons the reform consists merely in discarding certain unwholesome foods. They do not understand clearly the principles of health, and their tables, still loaded with harmful dainties, are far from being an example of Christian temperance and moderation.

Another class, in their desire to set a right example, go to the opposite extreme. Some are unable to obtain the most desirable foods, and, instead of using such things as would best supply the lack, they adopt an impoverished diet. Their food does not supply the elements needed to make good blood. Their health suffers, their usefulness is impaired, and their example tells against, rather than in favor of, reform in diet.

Others think that since health requires a simple diet, there need be little care in the selection or the preparation of food. Some restrict themselves to a very meager diet, not having sufficient variety to supply the needs of the system, and they suffer in consequence.

Those who have but a partial understanding of the principles of reform are often the most rigid, not only in carrying out their views themselves, but in urging them on their families and their neighbors. The effect of their mistaken reforms, as seen in their own ill-health, and their efforts to force their views upon others, give many a false idea of dietetic reform, and lead them to reject it altogether.

Those who understand the laws of health and who are governed by principle, will shun the extremes, both of indulgence and of restriction. Their diet is chosen, not for the mere gratification of appetite, but for the upbuilding of the body. They seek to preserve every power in the best condition for highest service to God and man. The appetite is under the control of reason and conscience, and they are rewarded with health of body and mind. While they do not urge their views offensively upon others, their example is a testimony in favor of right principles. These persons have a wide influence for good.

There is real common sense in dietetic reform. The subject should be studied broadly and deeply, and no one should criticize others because their practice is not, in all things, in harmony with his own. It is impossible to make an unvarying rule to regulate everyone's habits, and no one should think himself a criterion for all. Not all can eat the same things. Foods that are palatable and wholesome to one person may be distasteful, and even harmful, to another. Some cannot use milk, while others thrive on it. Some persons cannot digest peas and beans; others find them wholesome. For some the coarser grain preparations are good food, while others cannot use them.

Those who live in new countries or in poverty-stricken districts, where fruits and nuts are scarce, should not be urged to exclude milk and eggs from their dietary. It is true that persons in full flesh and in whom the animal passions are strong need to avoid the use of stimulating foods. Especially in families of children who are given to sensual habits, eggs should not be used. But in the case of persons whose blood-making organs are feeble,–especially if other foods to supply the needed elements cannot be obtained,–milk and eggs should not be wholly discarded. Great care should be taken, however, to obtain milk from healthy cows, and eggs from healthy fowls, that are well fed and well cared for; and the eggs should be so cooked as to be most easily digested.

The diet reform should be progressive. As disease in animals increases, the use of milk and eggs will become more and more unsafe. An effort should be made to supply their place with other things that are healthful and inexpensive. The people everywhere should be taught how to cook without milk and eggs, so far as possible, and yet have their food wholesome and palatable.

The practice of eating but two meals a day is generally found a benefit to health; yet under some circumstances persons may require a third meal. This should, however, if taken at all, be very light, and of food most easily digested. "Crackers"–the English biscuit–or zwieback, and fruit, or cereal coffee, are the foods best suited for the evening meal.

Some are continually anxious lest their food, however simple and healthful, may hurt them. To these let me say, Do not think that your food will injure you; do not think about it at all. Eat according to your best judgment; and when you have asked the Lord to bless the food for the strengthening of your body, believe that He hears your prayer, and be at rest.

Because principle requires us to discard those things that irritate the stomach and impair health, we should remember that an impoverished diet produces poverty of the blood. Cases of disease most difficult to cure result from this cause. The system is not sufficiently nourished, and dyspepsia and general debility are the result. Those who use such a diet are not always compelled by poverty to do so, but they choose it through ignorance or negligence, or to carry out their erroneous ideas of reform.

God is not honored when the body is neglected or abused and is thus unfitted for His service. To care for the body by providing for it food that is relishable and strengthening is one of the first duties of the householder. It is far better to have less expensive clothing and furniture than to stint the supply of food.

Some householders stint the family table in order to provide expensive entertainment for visitors. This is unwise. In the entertainment of guests there should be greater simplicity. Let the needs of the family have first attention.

Unwise economy and artificial customs often prevent the exercise of hospitality where it is needed and would be a blessing. The regular supply of food for our tables should be such that the unexpected guest can be made welcome without burdening the housewife to make extra preparation.

All should learn what to eat and how to cook it. Men, as well as women, need to understand the simple, healthful preparation of food. Their business often calls them where they cannot obtain wholesome food; then, if they have a knowledge of cookery, they can use it to good purpose.

Carefully consider your diet. Study from cause to effect. Cultivate self-control. Keep appetite under the control of reason. Never abuse the stomach by overeating, but do not deprive yourself of the wholesome, palatable food that health demands.

The narrow ideas of some would-be health reformers have been a great injury to the cause of hygiene. Hygienists should remember that dietetic reform will be judged, to a great degree, by the provision they make for their tables; and instead of taking a course that will bring discredit upon it, they should so exemplify its principles as to commend them to candid minds. There is a large class who will oppose any reform movement, however reasonable, if it places a restriction on the appetite. They consult taste instead of reason or the laws of health. By this class, all who leave the beaten track of custom and advocate reform will be accounted radical, no matter how consistent their course. That these persons may have no ground for criticism, hygienists should not try to see how different they can be from others, but should come as near to them as possible without the sacrifice of principle.

When those who advocate hygienic reform go to extremes, it is no wonder that many who regard these persons as representing health principles reject the reform altogether. These extremes frequently do more harm in a short time than could be undone by a lifetime of consistent living.

Hygienic reform is based upon principles that are broad and far-reaching, and we should not belittle it by narrow views and practices. But no one should permit opposition or ridicule, or a desire to please or influence others, to turn him from true principles, or cause him lightly to regard them. Those who are governed by principle will be firm and decided in standing for the right; yet in all their associations they will manifest a generous, Christlike spirit and true moderation.

STIMULANTS AND NARCOTICS

Under the head of stimulants and narcotics is classed a great variety of articles that, altogether used as food or drink, irritate the stomach, poison the blood, and excite the nerves. Their use is a positive evil. Men seek the excitement of stimulants, because, for the time, the results are agreeable. But there is always a reaction. The use of unnatural stimulants always tends to excess, and it is an active agent in promoting physical degeneration and decay.

CONDIMENTS

In this fast age, the less exciting the food, the better. Condiments are injurious in their nature. Mustard, pepper, spices, pickles, and other things of a like character, irritate the stomach and make the blood feverish and impure. The inflamed condition of the drunkard's stomach is often pictured as illustrating the effect of alcoholic liquors. A similarly inflamed condition is produced by the use of irritating condiments. Soon ordinary food does not satisfy the appetite. The system feels a want, a craving, for something more stimulating.

TEA AND COFFEE

Tea acts as a stimulants and, to a certain extent, produces intoxication. The action of coffee and many other popular drinks is similar. The first effect is exhilarating. The nerves of the stomach are excited; these convey irritation to the brain, and this in turn is aroused to impart increased action to the heart and short-lived energy to the entire system. Fatigue is forgotten; the strength seems to be increased. The intellect is aroused, the imagination becomes more vivid.

Because of these results, many suppose that their tea or coffee is doing them great good. But this is a mistake. Tea and coffee do not nourish the system. Their effect is produced before there has been time for digestion and assimilation, and what seems to be strength is only nervous excitement. When the influence of the stimulant is gone, the unnatural force abates, and the result is a corresponding degree of languor and debility.

The continued use of these nerve irritants is followed by headache, wakefulness, palpitation of the heart, indigestion, trembling, and many other evils; for they wear away the life forces. Tired nerves need rest and quiet instead of stimulation and overwork. Nature needs time to recuperate her exhausted energies. When her forces are goaded on by the use of stimulants, more will be accomplished for a time; but, as the system becomes debilitated by their constant use, it gradually becomes more difficult to rouse the energies to the desired point. The demand for stimulants becomes more difficult to control, until the will is overborne and there seems to be no power to deny the unnatural craving. Stronger and still stronger stimulants are called for, until exhausted nature can no longer respond.

THE TOBACCO HABIT

Tobacco is a slow, insidious, but most malignant poison. In whatever form it is used, it tells upon the constitution; it is all the more dangerous because its effects are slow and at first hardly perceptible. It excites and then paralyzes the nerves. It weakens and clouds the brain. Often it affects the nerves in a more powerful manner than does intoxicating drink. It is more subtle, and its effects are difficult to eradicate from the system. Its use excites a thirst for strong drink and in many cases lays the foundation for the liquor habit.

The use of tobacco is inconvenient, expensive, uncleanly, defiling to the user, and offensive to others. Its devotees are encountered everywhere. You rarely pass through a crowd but some smoker puffs his poisoned breath in your face. It is unpleasant and unhealthful to remain in a railway car or in a room where the atmosphere is laden with the fumes of liquor and tobacco. Though men persist in using these poisons themselves, what right have they to defile the air that others must breathe?

Among children and youth the use of tobacco is working untold harm. The unhealthful practices of past generations affect the children and youth of today. Mental inability, physical weakness, disordered nerves, and unnatural cravings are transmitted as a legacy from parents to children. And the same practices, continued by the children, are increasing and perpetuating the evil results. To this cause in no small degree is owing the physical, mental, and moral deterioration which is becoming such a cause of alarm.

Boys begin the use of tobacco at a very early age. The habit thus formed when body and mind are especially susceptible to its effects, undermines the physical strength, dwarfs the body, stupefies the mind, and corrupts the morals.

But what can be done to teach children and youth the evils of a practice of which parents, teachers, and ministers set them the example? Little boys, hardly emerged from babyhood, may be seen smoking their cigarettes. If one speaks to them about it, they say, "My father uses tobacco." They point to the minister or the Sunday-school superintendent and say, "Such a man smokes; what harm for me to do as he does?" Many workers in the temperance cause are addicted to the use of tobacco. What power can such persons have to stay the progress of intemperance?

I appeal to those who profess to believe and obey the word of God: Can you as Christians indulge a habit that is paralyzing your intellect and robbing you of power rightly to estimate eternal realities? Can you consent daily to rob God of service which is His due, and to rob your fellow men, both of service you might render and of the power of example?

Have you considered your responsibility as God's stewards, for the means in your hands? How much of the Lord's money do you spend for tobacco? Reckon up what you have thus spent during your lifetime. How does the amount consumed by this defiling lust compare with what you have given for the relief of the poor and the spread of the gospel?

No human being needs tobacco, but multitudes are perishing for want of the [money] that by its use is worse than wasted. Have you not been misappropriating the Lord's goods? Have you not been guilty of robbery toward God and your fellow men? "Know ye not that . .. ye are not your own? For ye are bought with a price: therefore glorify God in your body, and in your spirit, which are God's." 1 Corinthians 6:19, 20 See Proverbs 20:1; 23:29-32.

Never was traced by human hand a more vivid picture of the debasement and the slavery of the victim of intoxicating drink. Enthralled, degraded, even when awakened to a sense of his misery, he has no power to break from the snare; he "will seek it yet again." Verse 35.

No argument is needed to show the evil effects of intoxicants on the drunkard. The bleared, besotted wrecks of humanity–souls for whom Christ died, and over whom angels weep–are everywhere. They are a blot on our boasted civilization. They are the shame and curse and peril of every land.

And who can picture the wretchedness, the agony, the despair, that are hidden in the drunkard's home? Think of the wife, often delicately reared, sensitive, cultured, and refined, linked to one whom drink transforms into a sot or a demon. Think of the children, robbed of home comforts, education, and training, living in terror of him who should be their pride and protection, thrust into the world, bearing the brand of shame, often with the hereditary curse of the drunkard's thirst.

Think of the frightful accidents that are every day occurring through the influence of drink. Some official on a railway train neglects to heed a signal or misinterprets an order. On goes the train; there is a collision, and many lives are lost. Or a steamer is run aground, and passengers and crew find a watery grave. When the matter is investigated, it is found that someone at an important post was under the influence of drink. To what extent can one indulge the liquor habit and be safely trusted with the lives of human beings? He can be trusted only as he totally abstains.

THE MILDER INTOXICANTS

Persons who have inherited an appetite for unnatural stimulants should by no means have wine, beer, or cider in their sight, or within their reach; for this keeps the temptation constantly before them. Regarding sweet cider as harmless, many have no scruples in purchasing it freely. But it remains sweet for a short time only; then fermentation begins. The sharp taste which it then acquires makes it all the more acceptable to many palates, and the user is loath to admit that it has become hard, or fermented.

There is danger to health in the use of even sweet cider as ordinarily produced. If people could see what the microscope reveals in regard to the cider they buy, few would be willing to drink it. Often those who manufacture cider for the market are not careful as to the condition of the fruit used, and the juice of wormy and decayed apples is expressed. Those who would not think of using the poisonous, rotten apples in any other way, will drink the cider made from them, and call it a luxury; but the microscope shows that even when fresh from the press, this pleasant beverage is wholly unfit for use. Intoxication is just as really produced by wine, beer, and cider as by stronger drinks. The use of these drinks awakens the taste for those that are stronger, and thus the liquor habit is established. Moderate drinking is the school in which men are educated for the drunkard's career. Yet so insidious is the work of these milder stimulants that the highway to drunkenness is entered before the victim suspects his danger.

Some who are never considered really drunk are always under the influence of mild intoxicants. They are feverish, unstable in mind, unbalanced. Imagining themselves secure, they go on and on, until every barrier is broken down, every principle sacrificed. The strongest resolutions are undermined, the highest considerations are not sufficient to keep the debased appetite under the control of reason.

The Bible nowhere sanctions the use of intoxicating wine. The wine that Christ made from water at the marriage feast of Cana was the pure juice of the grape. This is the "new wine. . . found in the cluster," of which the Scripture says, "Destroy it not; for a blessing is in it." Isaiah 65:8.

It was Christ who, in the Old Testament, gave the warning to Israel, "Wine is a mocker, strong drink is raging: and whosoever is deceived thereby is not wise." Proverbs 20:1. He Himself provided no such beverage. Satan tempts men to indulgence that will becloud reason and benumb the spiritual perceptions, but Christ teaches us to bring the lower nature into subjection. He never places before men that which would be a temptation. His whole life was an example of self-denial. It was to break the power of appetite that in the forty days' fast in the wilderness He suffered in our behalf the severest test that humanity could endure. It was Christ who directed that John the Baptist should drink neither wine nor strong drink. It was He who enjoined similar abstinence upon the wife of Manoah. Christ did not contradict His own teaching. The unfermented wine that He provided for the wedding guests was a wholesome and refreshing drink. This is the wine that was used by our Saviour and His disciples in the first Communion. It is the wine that should always be used on the Communion table as a symbol of the Saviour's blood. The sacramental service is designed to be soul-refreshing and life-giving. There is to be connected with it nothing that could minister to evil.

In the light of what the Scriptures, nature, and reason teach concerning the use of intoxicants, how can Christians engage in the raising of hops for beer making, or in the manufacture of wine or cider for the market? If they love their neighbor as themselves, how can they help to place in his way that which will be a snare to him?

Often intemperance begins in the home. By the use of rich, unhealthful food the digestive organs are weakened, and a desire is created for food that is still more stimulating. Thus the appetite is educated to crave continually something stronger. The demand for stimulants becomes more frequent and more difficult to resist. The system becomes more or less filled with poison, and the more debilitated it becomes, the greater is the desire for these things. One step in the wrong direction prepares the way for another. Many who would not be guilty of placing on their table wine or liquor of any kind will load their table with food which creates such a thirst for strong drink that to resist the temptation is almost impossible. Wrong habits of eating and drinking destroy the health and prepare the way for drunkenness.

There would soon be little necessity for temperance crusades if in the youth who form and fashion society, right principles in regard to temperance could be implanted. Let parents begin a crusade against intemperance at their own firesides, in the principles they teach their children to follow from infancy, and they may hope for success.

There is work for mothers in helping their children to form correct habits and pure tastes. Educate the appetite; teach the children to abhor stimulants. Bring your children up to have moral stamina to resist the evil that surrounds them. Teach them that they are not to be swayed by others, that they are not to yield to strong influences, but to influence others for good.

Great efforts are made to put down intemperance; but there is much effort that is not directed to the right point. The advocates of temperance reform should be awake to the evils resulting from the use of unwholesome food, condiments, tea, and coffee. We bid all temperance workers Godspeed; but we invite them to look more deeply into the cause of the evil they war against and to be sure that they are consistent in reform.

It must be kept before the people that the right balance of the mental and moral powers depends in a great degree on the right condition of the physical system. All narcotics and unnatural stimulants that enfeeble and degrade the physical nature tend to lower the tone of the intellect and morals. Intemperance lies at the foundation of the moral depravity of the world. By the indulgence of perverted appetite, man loses his power to resist temptation.

Temperance reformers have a work to do in educating the people in these lines. Teach them that health, character, and even life, are endangered by the use of stimulants, which excite the exhausted energies to unnatural, spasmodic action.

In relation to tea, coffee, tobacco, and alcoholic drinks, the only safe course is to touch not, taste not, handle not. The tendency of tea, coffee, and similar drinks is in the same direction as that of alcoholic liquor and tobacco, and in some cases the habit is as difficult to break as it is for the drunkard to give up intoxicants. Those who attempt to leave off these stimulants will for a time feel a loss and will suffer without them. But by persistence they will overcome the craving and cease to feel the lack. Nature may require a little time to recover from the abuse she has suffered; but give her a chance, and she will again rally and perform her work nobly and well.

LIQUOR SALES AND PROHIBITION

"Woe unto him that buildeth his house by unrighteousness, and his chambers by wrong; . . . that saith, I will build me a wide house and large chambers, and cutteth him out windows; and it is ceiled with cedar, and painted with vermilion. Shalt thou reign, because thou closest thyself in cedar? . . . Thine eyes and thine heart are not but for thy covetousness, and for to shed innocent blood, and for oppression, and for violence, to do it." Jeremiah 22:13-17.

THE WORK OF THE LIQUOR SELLER

This scripture pictures the work of those who manufacture and who sell intoxicating liquor. Their business means robbery. For the money they receive, no equivalent is returned. Every dollar they add to their gains has brought a curse to the spender.

With a liberal hand, God has bestowed His blessings upon men. If His gifts were wisely used, how little the world would know of poverty or distress! It is the wickedness of men that turns His blessings into a curse. It is through the greed of gain and the lust of appetite that the grains and fruits given for our sustenance are converted into poisons that bring misery and ruin.

Every year millions upon millions of gallons of intoxicating liquors are consumed. Millions upon millions of dollars are spent in buying wretchedness, poverty, disease, degradation, lust, crime, and death. For the sake of gain, the liquor seller deals out to his victims that which corrupts and destroys mind and body. He entails on the drunkard's family poverty and wretchedness.

When his victim is dead, the rum seller's exactions do not cease. He robs the widow and brings children to beggary. He does not hesitate to take the very necessaries of life from the destitute family, to pay the drink bill of the husband and father. The cries of the suffering children, the tears of the agonized mother, serve only to exasperate him. What is it to him if these suffering ones starve? What is it to him if they, too, are driven to degradation and ruin? He grows rich on the pittances of those whom he is leading to perdition.

Houses of prostitution, dens of vice, criminal courts, prisons, almshouses, insane asylums, hospitals, all are, to a great degree, filled as a result of the liquor seller's work. Like the mystic Babylon of the Apocalypse, he is dealing in "slaves, and souls of men." Behind the liquor seller stands the mighty destroyer of souls, and every art which earth or hell can devise is employed to draw human beings under his power. In the city and the country, on the railway trains, on the great steamers, in places of business, in the halls of pleasure, in the medical dispensary, even in the church, on the sacred Communion table, his traps are set. Nothing is left undone to create and to foster the desire for intoxicants. On almost every corner stands the public house, with its brilliant lights, its welcome and good cheer, inviting the working man, the wealthy idler, and the unsuspecting youth.

In private lunchrooms and fashionable resorts, ladies are supplied with popular drinks, under some pleasing name, that are really intoxicants. For the sick and the exhausted, there are the widely advertised bitters, consisting largely of alcohol.

To create the liquor appetite in little children, alcohol is introduced into confectionery. Such confectionery is sold in the shops. And by the gift of these candies the liquor seller entices children into his resorts.

Day by day, month by month, year by year, the work goes on. Fathers and husbands and brothers, the stay and hope and pride of the nation, are steadily passing into the liquor dealer's haunts, to be sent back wrecked and ruined.

More terrible still, the curse is striking the very heart of the home. More and more, women are forming the liquor habit. In many a household, little children, even in the innocence and helplessness of babyhood, are in daily peril through the neglect, the abuse, the vileness of drunken mothers. Sons and daughters are growing up under the shadow of this terrible evil. What outlook for their future but that they will sink even lower than their parents?

From so-called Christian lands the curse is carried to the regions of idolatry. The poor, ignorant savages are taught the use of liquor. Even among the heathen, men of intelligence recognize and protest against it as a deadly poison; but in vain have they sought to protect their lands from its ravages. By civilized peoples, tobacco, liquor, and opium are forced upon the heathen nations. The ungoverned passions of the savage, stimulated by drink, drag him down to degradation before unknown, and it becomes an almost hopeless undertaking to send missionaries to these lands.

Through their contact with peoples who should have given them a knowledge of God, the heathen are led into vices which are proving the destruction of whole tribes and races. And in the dark places of the earth the men of civilized nations are hated because of this.

THE RESPONSIBILITY OF THE CHURCH

The liquor interest is a power in the world. It has on its side the combined strength of money, habit, appetite. Its power is felt even in the church. Men whose money has been made, directly or indirectly, in the liquor traffic, are members of churches, "in good and regular standing." Many of them give liberally to popular charities. Their contributions help to support the enterprises of the church and to sustain its ministers. They command the consideration shown to the money power. Churches that accept such members are virtually sustaining the liquor traffic. Too often the minister has not the courage to stand for the right. He does not declare to his people what God has said concerning the work of the liquor seller. To speak plainly would mean the offending of his congregation, the sacrifice of his popularity, the loss of his salary.

But above the tribunal of the church is the tribunal of God. He who declared to the first murderer, "The voice of thy brother's blood crieth unto Me from the ground" (Genesis 4:10), will not accept for His altar the gifts of the liquor dealer. His anger is kindled against those who attempt to cover their guilt with a cloak of liberality. Their money is stained with blood. A curse is upon it. See Isaiah 1:11-15.

The drunkard is capable of better things. He has been entrusted with talents with which to honor God and bless the world; but his fellow men have laid a snare for his soul and built themselves up by his degradation. They have lived in luxury while the poor victims whom they have robbed, lived in poverty and wretchedness. But God will require for this at the hand of him who has helped to speed the drunkard on to ruin. He who rules in the heavens has not lost sight of the first cause or the last effect of drunkenness. He who has a care for the sparrow and clothes the grass of the field, will not pass by those who have been formed in His own image, purchased with His own blood, and pay no heed to their cries. God marks all this wickedness that perpetuates crime and misery.

The world and the church may have approval for the man who has gained wealth by degrading the human soul. They may smile upon him by whom men are led down step by step in the path of shame and degradation. But God notes it all and renders a just judgment. The liquor seller may be termed by the world a good businessman; but the Lord says, "Woe unto him." He will be charged with the hopelessness, the misery, the suffering, brought into the world by the liquor traffic. He will have to answer for the want and woe of the mothers and children who have suffered for food and clothing and shelter, and who have buried all hope and joy. He will have to answer for the souls he has sent unprepared into eternity. And those who sustain the liquor seller in his work are sharers in his guilt. To them God says, "Your hands are full of blood."

LIQUOR LICENSE LAWS

The licensing of the liquor traffic is advocated by many as tending to restrict the drink evil. But the licensing of the traffic places it under the protection of law. The government sanctions its existence, and thus fosters the evil which it professes to restrict. Under the protection of license laws, breweries, distilleries, and wineries are planted all over the land, and the liquor seller plies his work beside our very doors.

Often he is forbidden to sell intoxicants to one who is drunk or who is known to be a confirmed drunkard; but the work of making drunkards of the youth goes steadily forward. Upon the creating of the liquor appetite in the youth the very life of the traffic depends. The youth are led on, step by step, until the liquor habit is established and the thirst is created that at any cost demands satisfaction. Less harmful would it be to grant liquor to the confirmed drunkard, whose ruin, in most cases, is already determined, than to permit the flower of our youth to be lured to destruction through this terrible habit.

By the licensing of the liquor traffic, temptation is kept constantly before those who are trying to reform. Institutions have been established where the victims of intemperance may be helped to overcome their appetite. This is a noble work; but so long as the sale of liquor is sanctioned by law, the intemperate receive little benefit from inebriate asylums. They cannot remain there always. They must again take their place in society. The appetite for intoxicating drink, though subdued, is not wholly destroyed; and when temptation assails them, as it does on every hand, they too often fall an easy prey.

The man who has a vicious beast and who, knowing its disposition, allows it liberty, is by the laws of the land held accountable for the evil the beast may do. In the laws given to Israel the Lord directed that when a beast known to be vicious caused the death of a human being, the life of the owner should pay the price of his carelessness or malignity. On the same principle the government that licenses the liquor seller should be held responsible for the results of his traffic. And if it is a crime worthy of death to give liberty to a vicious beast, how much greater is the crime of sanctioning the work of the liquor seller!

Licenses are granted on the plea that they bring a revenue to the public treasury. But what is this revenue when compared with the enormous expense incurred for the criminals, the insane, the paupers, that are the fruit of the liquor traffic! A man under the influence of liquor commits a crime; he is brought into court; and those who legalized the traffic are forced to deal with the result of their own work. They authorized the sale of a draft that would make a sane man mad; and now it is necessary for them to send the man to prison or to the gallows, while often his wife and children are left destitute to become the charge of the community in which they live.

Considering only the financial aspect of the question, what folly it is to tolerate such a business! But what revenue can compensate for the loss of human reason, for the defacing and deforming of the image of God in man, for the ruin of children, reduced to pauperism and degradation, to perpetuate in their children the evil tendencies of their drunken fathers?

PROHIBITION

The man who has formed the habit of using intoxicants is in a desperate situation. His brain is diseased, his will power is weakened. So far as any power in himself is concerned, his appetite is uncontrollable. He cannot be reasoned with or persuaded to deny himself. Drawn into the dens of vice, one who has resolved to quit drink is led to seize the glass again, and with the first taste of the intoxicant every good resolution is overpowered, every vestige of will destroyed. One taste of the maddening draft, and all thought of its results has vanished. The heartbroken wife is forgotten. The debauched father no longer cares that his children are hungry and naked. By legalizing the traffic, the law gives its sanction to this downfall of the soul and refuses to stop the trade that fills the world with evil.

Must this always continue? Will souls always have to struggle for victory, with the door of temptation wide open before them? Must the curse of intemperance forever rest like a blight upon the civilized world? Must it continue to sweep, every year, like a devouring fire over thousands of happy homes? When a ship is wrecked in sight of shore, people do not idly look on. They risk their lives in the effort to rescue men and women from a watery grave. How much greater the demand for effort in rescuing them from the drunkard's fate!

It is not the drunkard and his family alone who are imperiled by the work of the liquor seller, nor is the burden of taxation the chief evil which his traffic brings on the community. We are all woven together in the web of humanity. The evil that befalls any part of the great human brotherhood brings peril to all.

Many a man who through love of gain or ease would have nothing to do with restricting the liquor traffic has found, too late, that the traffic had to do with him. He has seen his own children besotted and ruined. Lawlessness runs riot. Property is in danger. Life is unsafe. Accidents by sea and by land multiply. Diseases that breed in the haunts of filth and wretchedness make their way to lordly and luxurious homes. Vices fostered by the children of debauchery and crime infect the sons and daughters of refined and cultured households.

There is no man whose interests the liquor traffic does not imperil. There is no man who for his own safeguard should not set himself to destroy it.

Above all other places having to do with secular interests only, legislative halls and courts of justice should be free from the curse of intemperance. Governors, senators, representatives, judges, men who enact and administer a nation's laws, men who hold in their hands the lives, the fair fame, the possessions of their fellows, should be men of strict temperance. Only thus can their minds be clear to discriminate between right and wrong. Only thus can they possess firmness of principle, and wisdom to administer justice and to show mercy. But how does the record stand? How many of these men have their minds beclouded, their sense of right and wrong confused, by strong drink! How many are the oppressive laws enacted, how many the innocent persons condemned to death, through the injustice of drinking lawmakers, witnesses, jurors, lawyers, and even judges! Many there are, "mighty to drink wine," and "men of strength to mingle strong drink," "that call evil good, and good evil;" that "justify the wicked for reward, and take away the righteousness of the righteous from him!" Of such God says:

"Woe unto them.. . .
As the fire devoureth the stubble,
And the flame consumeth the chaff,
So their root shall be as rottenness,
And their blossom shall go up as dust:
Because they have cast away the law of the Lord of hosts,
And despised the word of the Holy One of Israel.

Isaiah 5:22-24.

The honor of God, the stability of the nation, the well-being of the community, of the home, and of the individual, demand that every possible effort be made in arousing the people to the evil of intemperance. Soon we shall see the result of this terrible evil as we do not see it now. Who will put forth a determined effort to stay the work of destruction? As yet the contest has hardly begun. Let an army be formed to stop the sale of the drugged liquors that are making men mad. Let the danger from the liquor traffic be made plain and a public sentiment be created that shall demand its prohibition. Let the drink-maddened men be given an opportunity to escape from their thralldom. Let the voice of the nation demand of its lawmakers that a stop be put to this infamous traffic. See Proverbs 24:11, 12; Jeremiah 13:21.

THE SECRET OF HAPPINESS

It is morning on the Sea of Galilee. Jesus and His disciples have come to shore after a tempestuous night on the water, and the light of the rising sun touches sea and land as with the benediction of peace. But as they step upon the beach they are greeted with a sight more terrible than the storm-tossed sea. From some hiding place among the tombs two madmen rush upon them as if to tear them in pieces. Hanging about these men are parts of chains which they have broken in escaping from confinement. Their flesh is torn and bleeding, their eyes glare out from their long and matted hair, the very likeness of humanity seems to have been blotted out. They look more like wild beasts than like men.

The disciples and their companions flee in terror; but presently they notice that Jesus is not with them, and they turn to look for Him. He is standing where they left Him. He who stilled the tempest, who has before met Satan and conquered him, does not flee before these demons. When the men, gnashing their teeth and foaming at the mouth, approach Him, Jesus raises that hand which has beckoned the waves to rest, and the men can come no nearer. They stand before Him, raging but helpless.

With authority He bids the unclean spirits come out of them. The unfortunate men realize that One is near who can save them from the tormenting demons. They fall at the Saviour's feet to entreat His mercy; but when their lips are opened, the demons speak through them, crying, "What have we to do with Thee, Jesus, Thou Son of God? art Thou come hither to torment us?" Matthew 8:29.

The evil spirits are forced to release their victims, and a wonderful change comes over the demoniacs. Light shines into their minds. Their eyes beam with intelligence. The countenances so long deformed into the image of Satan become suddenly mild, the blood-stained hands are quiet, and the men lift their voices in praise to God.

Meanwhile the demons, cast out from their human habitation, have entered into the swine and driven them to destruction. The keepers of the swine hurry away to publish the news, and the whole population flock to meet Jesus. The two demoniacs have been the terror of the country. Now these men are clothed and in their right mind, sitting at the feet of Jesus, listening to His words, and glorifying the name of Him who has made them whole. But those who behold this wonderful scene do not rejoice. The loss of the swine seems to them of greater moment than the deliverance of these captives of Satan. In terror they throng about Jesus, beseeching Him to depart from them, and He complies, taking ship at once for the opposite shore.

Far different is the feeling of the restored demoniacs. They desire the companionship of their Deliverer. In His presence they feel secure from the demons that have tormented their lives and wasted their manhood. As Jesus is about to enter the boat they keep close to His side, kneel at His feet, and beg to remain near Him, where they may listen to His words. But Jesus bids them go home and tell what great things the Lord has done for them.

Here is a work for them to do–to go to a heathen home and tell of the blessings they have received from Jesus. It is hard for them to be separated from the Saviour. Great difficulties will beset them in association with their heathen countrymen. And their long isolation from society seems to have disqualified them for this work. But as soon as He points out their duty, they are ready to obey.

Not only did they tell their own households and neighbors about Jesus, but they went throughout Decapolis, everywhere declaring His power to save and describing how He had freed them from the demons.

Though the people of Gergesa had not received Jesus, He did not leave them to the darkness they had chosen. When they bade Him depart from them, they had not heard His words. They were ignorant of that which they were rejecting. Therefore He sent the light to them, and by those to whom they would not refuse to listen.

In causing the destruction of the swine, it was Satan's purpose to turn the people away from the Saviour and prevent the preaching of the gospel in that region. But this very occurrence roused the country as nothing else could have done, and directed attention to Christ. Though the Saviour Himself departed, the men whom He had healed remained as witnesses to His power. Those who had been mediums of the prince of darkness became channels of light, messengers of the Son of God. When Jesus returned to Decapolis, the people flocked about Him, and for three days thousands from all the surrounding country heard the message of salvation.

The two restored demoniacs were the first missionaries whom Christ sent to teach the gospel in the region of Decapolis. For a short time only, these men had listened to His words. Not one sermon from His lips had ever fallen upon their ears. They could not instruct the people as the disciples who had been daily with Christ were able to do. But they could tell what they knew; what they themselves had seen, and heard, and felt of the Saviour's power. This is what everyone can do whose heart has been touched by the grace of God. This is the witness for which our Lord calls, and for want of which the world is perishing.

The gospel is to be presented, not as a lifeless theory, but as a living force to change the life. God would have His servants bear testimony to the fact that through His grace men may possess Christlikeness of character and may rejoice in the assurance of His great love. He would have us bear testimony to the fact that He cannot be satisfied until all who will accept salvation are reclaimed and reinstated in their holy privileges as His sons and daughters.

Even those whose course has been most offensive to Him He freely accepts. When they repent, He imparts to them His divine Spirit, and sends them forth into the camp of the disloyal to proclaim His mercy. Souls that have been degraded into instruments of Satan are still, through the power of Christ, transformed into messengers of righteousness and are sent forth to tell how great things the Lord hath done for them and hath had compassion on them.

After the woman of Capernaum had been healed by the touch of faith, Jesus desired her to acknowledge the blessing she had received. The gifts which the gospel offers are not to be secured by stealth or enjoyed in secret. "Ye are My witnesses, saith the Lord, That I am God." Isaiah 43:12.

Our confession of His faithfulness is Heaven's chosen agency for revealing Christ to the world. We are to acknowledge His grace as made known through the holy men of old; but that which will be most effectual is the testimony of our own experience. We are witnesses for God as we reveal in ourselves the working of a power that is divine. Every individual has a life distinct from all others, and an experience differing essentially from theirs. God desires that our praise shall ascend to Him, marked with our own individuality. These precious acknowledgments to the praise of the glory of His grace, when supported by a Christlike life, have an irresistible power that works for the salvation of souls.

It is for our own benefit to keep every gift of God fresh in our memory. By this means faith is strengthened to claim and to receive more and more. There is greater encouragement for us in the least blessing we ourselves receive from God than in all the accounts we can read of the faith and experience of others. The soul that responds to the grace of God shall be like a watered garden. His health shall spring forth speedily; his light shall rise in obscurity, and the glory of the Lord shall be seen upon him. "What shall I render unto the Lord

For all His benefits toward me? I will take the cup of salvation, And call upon the name of the Lord. I will pay my vows unto the Lord, Yea, in the presence of all His people." "I will sing unto the Lord as long as I live: See Psalms 116:12-14, R.V.; 104:33, 34; 106:2; 105:1, 2 (A.R.V.), 2, 3; 63:3-7, A.R.V.; 56:11-13, A.R.V.; 71:22-24, 5, 6; 45:17.

"FREELY YE HAVE RECEIVED, FREELY GIVE."

The gospel invitation is not to be narrowed down and presented only to a select few, who, we suppose, will do us honor if they accept it. The message is to be given to all. When God blesses His children, it is not alone for their own sake, but for the world's sake. As He bestows His gifts on us, it is that we may multiply them by imparting.

The Samaritan woman who talked with Jesus at Jacob's well had no sooner found the Saviour than she brought others to Him. She proved herself a more effective missionary than His own disciples. The disciples saw nothing in Samaria to indicate that it was an encouraging field. Their thoughts were fixed upon a great work to be done in the future. They did not see that right around them was a harvest to be gathered. But through the woman whom they despised a whole cityful were brought to hear Jesus. She carried the light at once to her countrymen.

This woman represents the working of a practical faith in Christ. Every true disciple is born into the kingdom of God as a missionary. No sooner does he come to know the Saviour than he desires to make others acquainted with Him. The saving and sanctifying truth cannot be shut up in his heart. He who drinks of the living water becomes a fountain of life. The receiver becomes a giver. The grace of Christ in the soul is like a spring in the desert, welling up to refresh all, and making those who are ready to perish eager to drink of the water of life. In doing this work a greater blessing is received than if we work merely to benefit ourselves. It is in working to spread the good news of salvation that we are brought near to the Saviour.

Of those who receive His grace the Lord says:

"I will make them and the places round about My hill a blessing; and I will cause the shower to come down in its season; there shall be showers of blessing." Ezekiel 34:26, A.R.V.

"On the last day, the great day of the feast, Jesus stood and cried, saying, If any man thirst, let him come unto Me and drink. He that believeth on Me, as the scripture hath said, from within him shall flow rivers of living water." John 7:37, 38, A.R.V.

Those who receive are to impart to others. From every direction are coming calls for help. God calls upon men to minister gladly to their fellow men. Immortal crowns are to be won; the kingdom of heaven is to be gained; the world, perishing in ignorance, is to be enlightened.

"Say not ye, There are yet four months, and then cometh harvest? behold, I say unto you, Lift up your eyes, and look on the fields; for they are white already to harvest. And he that reapeth receiveth wages, and gathereth fruit unto life eternal." John 4:35, 36.

For three years the disciples had before them the wonderful example of Jesus. Day by day they walked and talked with Him, hearing His words of cheer to the weary and heavy-laden, and seeing the manifestations of His power in behalf of the sick and afflicted. When the time came for Him to leave them, He gave them grace and power to carry forward His work in His name. They were to shed abroad the light of His gospel of love and healing. And the Saviour promised that His presence would be always with them. Through the Holy Spirit He would be even nearer to them than when He walked visibly among men.

The work which the disciples did, we also are to do. Every Christian is to be a missionary. In sympathy and compassion we are to minister to those in need of help, seeking with unselfish earnestness to lighten the woes of suffering humanity.

All may find something to do. None need feel that there is no place where they can labor for Christ. The Saviour identifies Himself with every child of humanity. That we might become members of the heavenly family, He became a member of the earthly family. He is the Son of man, and thus a brother to every son and daughter of Adam. His followers are not to feel themselves detached from the perishing world around them. They are a part of the great web of humanity, and heaven looks upon them as brothers to sinners as well as to saints.

Millions upon millions of human beings, in sickness and ignorance and sin, have never so much as heard of Christ's love for them. Were our condition and theirs to be reversed, what would we desire them to do for us? All this, so far as lies in our power, we are to do for them. Christ's rule of life by which every one of us must stand or fall in the judgment is, "Whatsoever ye would that men should do to you, do ye even so to them." Matthew 7:12.

By all that has given us advantage over another,–be it education and refinement, nobility of character, Christian training, religious experience,–we are in debt to those less favored; and, so far as lies in our power, we are to minister unto them. If we are strong, we are to stay up the hands of the weak.

Angels of glory that do always behold the face of the Father in heaven, joy in ministering to His little ones. Angels are ever present where they are most needed, with those who have the hardest battles with self to fight, and whose surroundings are the most discouraging. Weak and trembling souls who have many objectionable traits of character are their special charge. That which selfish hearts would regard as humiliating service, ministering to those who are wretched and in every way inferior in character, is the work of the pure, sinless beings from the courts above.

Jesus did not consider heaven a place to be desired while we were lost. He left the heavenly courts for a life of reproach and insult, and a death of shame. He who was rich in heaven's priceless treasure became poor, that through His poverty we might be rich. We are to follow in the path He trod.

He who becomes a child of God should henceforth look upon

himself as a link in the chain let down to save the world, one with Christ in His plan of mercy, going forth with Him to seek and save the lost.

Many feel that it would be a great privilege to visit the scenes of Christ's life on earth, to walk where He trod, to look upon the lake beside which He loved to teach, and the hills and valleys on which His eyes so often rested. But we need not go to Nazareth, to Capernaum, or to Bethany, in order to walk in the steps of Jesus. We shall find His footprints beside the sickbed, in the hovels of poverty, in the crowded alleys of the great cities, and in every place where there are human hearts in need of consolation.

We are to feed the hungry, clothe the naked, and comfort the suffering and afflicted. We are to minister to the despairing, and to inspire hope in the hopeless.

The love of Christ, manifested in unselfish ministry, will be more effective in reforming the evildoer than will the sword or the court of justice. These are necessary to strike terror to the lawbreaker, but the loving missionary can do more than this. Often the heart that hardens under reproof will melt under the love of Christ.

The missionary can not only relieve physical maladies, but he can lead the sinner to the Great Physician, who can cleanse the soul from the leprosy of sin. Through His servants, God designs that the sick, the unfortunate, and those possessed of evil spirits shall hear His voice. Through His human agencies He desires to be a comforter such as the world knows not.

The Saviour has given His precious life in order to establish a church capable of ministering to the suffering, the sorrowful, and the tempted. A company of believers may be poor, uneducated, and unknown; yet in Christ they may do a work in the home, in the community, and even in "the regions beyond," whose results shall be as far-reaching as eternity.

To Christ's followers today, no less than to the first disciples, these words are spoken:

"All power is given unto Me in heaven and in earth. Go ye therefore, and teach all nations." "Go ye into all the world, and preach the gospel to every creature." Matthew 28:18, 19; Mark 16:15.

And for us also is the promise of His presence, "Lo, I am with you alway, even unto the end of the world." Matthew 28:20.

Today no curious multitudes flock to the desert places to see and hear the Christ. His voice is not heard in the busy streets. No cry sounds from the wayside, "Jesus of Nazareth passeth by." Luke 18:37.

Yet this word is true today. Christ walks unseen through our streets. With messages of mercy He comes to our homes. With all who are seeking to minister in His name, He waits to co-operate. He is in the midst of us, to heal and to bless, if we will receive Him.

"Thus saith Jehovah, In an acceptable time have I answered thee, and in a day of salvation have I helped thee; and I will preserve thee, and give thee for a covenant of the people, to raise up the land, to make them inherit the desolate heritages; saying to them that are bound, Go forth; to them that are in darkness, Show yourselves."

"How beautiful upon the mountains are the feet of him that bringeth good tidings, that publisheth peace;

That bringeth good tidings of good, that publisheth salvation; That saith unto Zion, Thy God reigneth!"

Isaiah 49:8, A.R.V.; 52:7.

"Break forth into joy, sing together, ye waste places:. . .

For the Lord hath comforted His people...

The Lord hath made bare His holy arm in the eyes of all the nations;

And all the ends of the earth shall see the salvation of our God." Verses 9, 10.

BLACK AMERICA'S LIVE-LONGER LIFESTYLE SELF-TEST

Take this self-test to see how closely you follow health principles proven to lengthen your life.

DIRECTIONS: For each item, circle the one number at the right that goes with the statement best describing your personal lifestyle. When finished, total all the numbers circled and find the scoring category into which you fit.

CIGARETTE SMOKING

A.	Never smoked, or quit more than 15 years ago	0
B.	Ex-smoker, quit 5 to 15 years ago	3
C.	Ex-smoker, quit within past 5 years	5
D.	Current smoker, less than 20 cigarettes per day	9
E.	Current smoker, 20 to 40 cigarettes per day	12
F.	Current smoker, more than 40 cigarettes per day	15

BEVERAGE CONSUMPTION (Alcohol, Coffee, etc.)

ALCOHOL: How many alcoholic drinks do you consume? A standard alcoholic drink contains 15 milliliters of ethanol, which is found in a 12-ounce can of beer, a 4-ounce glass of wine, or one shot of 100-proof bourbon.

A.	Never use alcohol	0
B.	Less than 1 per week	2
C.	1 to 6 per week	4
D.	1 per day	7
E.	2 to 3 per day	6
F.	More than 3 per day	8

WATER: How many glasses of water do you drink per day? (8 ounces per glass)

A.	More than 6	0
B.	4 to 6	1
C.	Less than 3	4

DIETARY INTAKE

Carefully note the portion sizes and include amounts used in all cooking and baking.

A.	TOTAL VEGETARIAN	0
	(no dairy, eggs or animal flesh)	
B.	LACTO -OVOVEGETARIAN(no animal flesh)	
	Cheeses (not cottage),1ounce (28 grams)	
	Seldom or never use	0
	Less than one serving per day	1
	More than one serving per day	2
	Milk (not low-fat/skim), 1 cup (244 grams)	
	Seldom or never use	0
	Less than one serving per day	1
	More than one serving per day	2
	Butter (real butter, not margarine), 1 tablespoon (14 grams)	
	Seldom or never use	0
	Less than one serving per week	1
	1 to 4 servings per week	3
	More than 4 servings per week	4
	Eggs (including yolk), 1 whole (50 grams)	
	Seldom or never use	0
	Less than one serving per week	1
	1 to 4 servings per week	2
	More than 4 servings per week	3
C.	OMNIVORE (animal flesh, dairy products, and plant foods)	
	Red flesh (beef, pork, lamb), 3 oz. (85 grams)	
	Seldom or never use	0
	Less than one serving per week	2
	1 to 4 servings per week	4
	More than 4 servings per week	6
	White flesh(fish, poultry) 3 oz. (85 grams)	
	Seldom or never use	0
	Less than one serving per day	1
	More than one serving per day	2

EXERCISE / FITNESS

Outside of your normal work or daily responsibilities, how often do you engage in exercise that moderately increases your breathing and heart rate for at least 20 continuous minutes—such as brisk walking, cycling, swimming, jogging, aerobic calisthenics, etc.?

A.	5 or more times per week	0
B.	3 to 4 times per week	1
C.	1 to 2 times per week	3
D.	Less than 1 time per week	7
E.	Seldom or never	10

DESIRABLE WEIGHT

How would you rate your body weight?

A.	Very close to ideal	0
B.	About 10 percent too high	2
C.	About 11 to 25 percent too high	5
D.	About 26 to 40 percent too high	7
E.	More than 40 percent too high	9

MENTAL/SOCIAL SPIRITUAL WELL-BEING

A. In general, how satisfied are you with your life?

Mostly satisfied	0
Partly satisfied	1
Mostly disappointed	3

B. How often do you get insufficient rest so that you are unable to function efficiently?

Less than weekly	0
Usually 1 night per week	1
2 or 3 nights per week	2
4 or more nights per week	3

C. How would you describe your emotional stress?

On the job:

Average or low stress	0
Much stress but can cope with it	1
Much stress and often feel unable to cope	3

At home:
Experience average or low stress 0
Experience much stress but am able to cope with it 1
Experience much stress and often feel unable to cope 3

D. Have you suffered a serious personal loss or misfortune in the past year (for example, divorce, separation, jail term, death of a close-person, job loss, disability)?
No 0
Yes, one serious loss 2
Yes, two or more serious losses 4

E. How many friends and relatives do you feel close to? (Your spouse and people you feel at ease with and can talk to about private matters, or call on for help.)
10 or more 0
5 to 9 1
1 to 4 2
None 3

F. How would you describe your relationship to God?
Close and growing 0
Less than desirable 2
Distant 4

PERSONAL FACTORS

A. How many deaths from heart disease or cancer have occured among close relatives before age 60? (parents,grandparents, aunts or uncles)
None 0
1 2
2 or more 5

B. What percent of the time do you use seat belts while driving or riding?
100 percent 0
50 to 99 percent 2
25 to 49 percent 4
Less than 25 percent of the time 6

C. How often do you see a physician for a physical checkup?

At least once per year	0
Only once every three years	2
Only once every five years	4

D. Your blood pressure* is:

Low or normal (less than 120/80 mm. Hg)	0
Borderline high (120/80 to 139/89)	3
Moderately high (140/90 to 159/94)	8
Very high (160/95 and higher)	12

* If you do not know your blood pressure, we highly recommend that you get it measured very soon. To estimate your blood pressure ranking, evaluate two lifestyle factors: body weight and salt intake. If your body weight and salt intake are at recommended levels, your risk of high blood pressure is greatly reduced. . The high potassium, low-sodium nature of the vegetarian diet aids in lowering blood pressure.

E. Your serum cholesterol **is:

Low (less than 180 mg./dl.)	0
Borderline high (180/199mg./dl.)	3
Moderately high (200-239 mg./dl.)	8
Very high (240 mg./dl. and higher)	12

**If you do not know your serum cholesterol, we highly recommend that you get it measured very soon. To complete the self-scoring test, you can estimate your serum cholesterol from the rankings above. The rankings include several lifestyle factors: saturated fat, dietary cholesterol, and dietary fiber intake; body weight; and regular exercise.

WHAT DOES YOUR SCORE MEAN?

The scoring system for this test is based on a broad construction of published research. The scoring range for each category is an approximation developed from evaluating the relative importance of the various lifestyle factors.

0 to 20 Excellent
Congratulations! You have an optimum-health lifestyle. Your potential for longevity and decreased risk of both heart disease and cancer is very high.

21 to 40 Very Good
If you find yourself in this category, you are probably only one or two lifestyle habits away from earning an excellent rating. You've already made wonderful progress— keep up the good work.

41 to 70 Fair
Many Americans will find themselves in this category. To fall in this category, you may have only one or two outstanding health problems. However, because of several less-than-optimum health practices in a wide variety of areas, your point total has reached an undesirable level. By gradually working on selected areas and improving health practices that you are presently motivated to act on, you can steadily progress to the "excellent" rating. Improved longevity and quality of life will be your reward.

71 to 95 Poor
Your risk of heart disease, cancer, and early death is high. Now is the time to sit down with your spouse or close friends and establish goals for changing your health behavior. There are many case histories of people who have turned their lifestyles completely around. The human body responds fruitfully to an improved lifestyle, often repairing some of the damage already done. For example, smokers who quit smoking eliminate all cigarette-related risk of heart disease after 15 years of abstinence.

96 to 140 Very Poor
Unusually high risk of early death from heart disease and/or cancer. You are urged to make an appointment with your physician to have a thorough checkup and to seek counseling for an improved lifestyle.

RESOLUTION

HEALTH EDUCATION FOR BLACK AMERICA

WHEREAS, In no place is there greater need of education in health principles than Black America because so many trangress the laws of health through ignorance and they need instruction,

WHEREAS, Medical science recognizes that emotional turmoil such as fear, sorrow, envy, resentment and hatred are disease-producing stresses which account for the majority of America's diseases,

WHEREAS, "Medical care alone will not eliminate the devastating impact of chronic disease on the disadvantaged, nor will it reduce... the rate of infant mortality or the burden of homicide and violence or many of the other health problems that are borne by the poor in our society alone,"

Louis W.Sullivan, M.D., Former Secretary,
U.S. Dept. of Health & Human Services

WHEREAS, God has pledged to Black America: "If thou wilt diligently hearken to the voice of the Lord thy God, and wilt do that which is right in his sight, and wilt give ear to his commandments, and keep all his statues, I will put none of these diseases upon thee, which I have brought upon the [Oppressors]: for I am the Lord that healeth thee." (Exodus 15:26);

WHEREAS the MINISTRY OF HEALING, published by Foy Institute Press, provides in simple language the same practical instruction and moral incentives as found in the Holy Bible for preventing disease and promoting health in Black America;

BLACK HEALTH RESOLUTION

BE IT THEREFORE RESOLVED,
that ____(Organization)
in the city of ______________________, __________, recognizes and adopts the MINISTRY OF HEALING FOR BLACK AMERICA as the Health Ministry Opportunity (HMO) of choice.

FURTHER, that we, the undersigned representatives of the above mentioned organization, hereby endorse the widest possible sale and distribution of the MINISTRY OF HEALING among its members and the larger community, in partial fulfillment of our responsibility to impress PEOPLE OF COLOR with the importance of making this knowledge a guide of life.

____

Signature *Title* *Date*

____

Signature *Title* *Date*

____

Signature *Title* *Date*

To establish an HMO through the assistance of a certified Lifestyle Trainer near you call:
Office of Regional Ministries in North America
205-830-5002

REPRINTS

To obtain additional copies or quantity rates for the Resolution or Live Longer Lifestyle Self-Test write:

FOY INSTITUTE PRESS
P.O.Box 25, Hagerstown, MD. 21741-0025